Grateful Testimonials

These are actual quotes from people who came upon the books, the blog, and the Facebook page - just in time to save them from becoming a victim of one of these Internet scams.

"I have an oak hutch for sale on Craiglist and received an email from Chris Hutson (dexme004@gmail.com). Thanks for sharing everyone's story. I would have been his next victim. Thanks!!"

"I'm an artist in Memphis who is very grateful for people like you who keep us informed on creeps like this. Thank you."

"Hi there, You have done an incredible job. I'll definitely digg it and personally recommend to my friends. I am confident they'll benefit from this website."

"Thank you for your efforts in fighting these jerks! And by the way, saw your work, beautiful!!!"

"Thanks for shedding light on this issue. I am a pretty paranoid person and am always wary of being a victim of scams like these."

"I read your description of their tactics and I see how they work now. Before yesterday, I didn't even realize art scammers existed, and I certainly had no idea how common they are! Thanks for helping to fight this, KatieMoe!"

"WOW, my suspicions have been confirmed, I had a Sandra Oche contact me about a Craigslist ad I ran for a room for rent with same letter from Vermont. EXCELLENT - you get my vote for Humanitarian of the Year!!"

Social Media Scams

Protect Yourself from Scams

on Facebook, Twitter, eBay & More

Volume 2 of Internet Scams Revealed Series

by

Kathleen McMahon

Disclaimer: The information I have written in this book is solely intended to provide a general understanding of the subject matter and to help readers assess whether they need to seek more detailed information. The material in this publication is not and must not be regarded as legal advice. Readers should seek their own legal advice where appropriate. I have endeavored to make sure that the information contained herein is accurate, however no liability is accepted for any loss or damage whatsoever that can be attributed to the reliance on any of that information.

Publisher: KTMObooks, 1450 Chestnut Street #102, San Francisco, CA 94123

ISBN: 978-1-938831-02-7

Library of Congress Control Number: 2012921575

This book is dedicated to all the individuals who tweet, re-tweet, update, upload, post, comment, share, recommend, check-in, pin, blog, join, chat, and tag. We, in all of our humanness, are more connected because of you.

Contents

INTRODUCTION

Internet scams are on the rise and there is plenty of evidence all around telling us this is so. I see news headlines about it every day. My question is why? Is it that internet scams have become more lucrative for scammers and so there are more of them? Or is it that the 'barrier to entry' of becoming a scammer is lower now so there are just more of them cutting into the money pie?

I read online today that a scammer can buy a phishing kit for 'dummies' (which provides instructions for how to send out phishing spam emails) for about $100, rent a botnet for about $5/hour and go ahead and push out more than 10,000 messages that look like they are coming from a known bank, UPS, or PayPal. So any lowlife with a little cash and time can get into the scamming business. I also think there is evidence scammers are actually stealing more total money than ever before – the average loss per person is going up. But it's hard to know for sure because so many victims do not report the crime. This tells me people are in dire need of being educated on how to avoid scams. And if you think it would never be you, let me say we are well past the days of thinking only dumb people or the very elderly fall for scams. I'm here to tell you *every* demographic falls for scams - from business owners to lawyers, seniors to the young, divorced to newly married, college graduates to laborers, artists to engineers, and everyone in between.

Here are some statistics revealing the scope of online crime from the Internet Crime Center (ICC) Report for 2011 (http://www.ic3.gov/media/annualreport/2011_ic3report.pdf). Note: complaints on this site are only registered if there is actual financial loss:

- It was the third year in a row that over 300,000 complaints were logged in one year (2009 was the peak so far). Over $485.3 million estimated loss from complaints in 2011.

- Victims came from these five top states – California, Florida, Texas, New York, and Ohio. Victims from California lost approximately $70.5 million in 2011. The average loss for all victims in 2011 was $4187 per victim.

- 51.76% of 2011 complaints were male.

- Highest number of complaints in 2011 came from the ages between 40-59 (43%) and seniors 60 and over represented only 14% of the complaints.

Top type of scams were:

1. Scammers posing as FBI to defraud victims.

2. Identity theft.

3. Advanced fee fraud – victims pay for something that doesn't exist or has no value.

4. Overpayment fraud – scammers overpaying with counterfeit check and asking victims to deposit and forward a portion (from their good money) to a third party via wire transfer.

A couple more important points:

- In romance scams, only 5600 complaints were filed in 2011 but total loss was $50.4 million, with women in the 50-59 age range experiencing the greatest loss.

- Work-at-home scams represented over $20 million dollars in losses in 2011.

There has got to be some way to reduce these numbers!

In Volume 1, *Top 10 Email Scams* (ISBN: 978-1-938831-00-3), I wrote about how I got into this battle. I also provide a supplemental resource guide, *Report Scams* (ASIN: B00BNIL6JM), that includes links and contact information for victims of Internet scams. I will be releasing more topics in this series, which I call, *Internet Scams Revealed.* You can sign up for my free newsletter at my website to keep updated on new releases.

I have two blogs, two Facebook pages, a Twitter account, and this book series dedicated to chipping away at the problem. There is power in the act of people posting warnings online to alert each other. It helps to bring these slimy guys (and women, too) out into the light where we see what they are doing. I invite you to do the same. When you get a scam email and you proudly now know and easily recognize it as a scam – go post it online somewhere so that others will be alerted to what it looks like. People tend to search on the person's name who has sent the email (scammers make up fake names but that's okay, they seem to use certain ones over and over again) and the email address (which is disposable, but that's okay, too – go ahead and post it online anyway). We can and will make a difference. This is what social media is all about. Power to the people. Welcome to the battle.

- Kathleen, Anti-Scam Samurai

CHAPTER 1
THE RISE OF SOCIAL MEDIA

Social Media is a term for a phenomenon that took content on the internet and transformed it from being a resource, much like a library, to a dynamic interactive conversation. The Internet went from being a place to look up and reference information from "trusted" sources to a reflection of what people are thinking about at any given second.

Before the Internet

Social media has been around since the beginning of computers but was a small aspect compared to static information presented as documents. Before the internet as we know it today, a fellow by the name of Roy Trubshaw invented a fantasy-based game called MUD1 (Multi User Dungeon, in homage to an offline game called Dungeons and Dragons) that multiple people could join in on using terminals connected to a DEC PDP-10 mainframe computer. That was 1978. By 1994, one could count over 400 MUDs on all different kinds of topics. They became virtual "interest groups" where users could connect with each other.

In 1988, Jarkko Oikarinen created Internet Relay Chat (IRC) while working at a university in Finland. It was its own network with its own server, one computer in the early days. It used the word "Internet" but that was long before the rise of the Internet as we know it today, which happened around 1993-94. IRC groups were established to share news, talk about software, and other issues. You had to install separate IRC software so that you could access these groups.

Usenet newsgroups began in 1980 and were in wide use as the Internet began to take off in the 1990's. They were the pre-cursor to forums. Also during this earlier period, BBS (Bulletin Board System) software programs began to appear on the scene. At the time, you would have to dial up to a particular BBS system and pay long distance phone charges, if they applied. Usenet used a store-and-forward system to move messages around, like BBSs. But with BBSs the "server" was dedicated and typically a single computer, whereas Usenet used distributed computers as servers, so moving messages around became a bit easier. The internet, as we know it today, took this idea of distributed servers and expanded it to such a degree that moving information and messages between one server and another on the Internet today seems almost instantaneous and seamless.

At the Beginning of the Internet

Programmers from Sun Microsystems created a programming language called Java in 1991. By 1995, chat rooms were created using this programming language. In 1993, the Mosaic web browser was created and suddenly the Internet had a visual appeal. At the same time, AOL (America Online) had developed its own proprietary "internet" system, separate from the Internet. By 1993, AOL created a "buddy list" for employees so that they could communicate instantly with other AOL employees, no matter where they were located.

The Internet "Bubble"

By 1995, we were really at the doorway of what came to be known as the "Internet Bubble", when an explosion of new businesses and services launched to stake their claim in the Wild West of this emerging environment.

By the time 1997 rolled around, AOL had very active private chat rooms and their proprietary AOL Instant Messenger (AIM) was available to all its subscribers. Yahoo wanted to offer something like AIM to non-AOL subscribers, so Yahoo Messenger was launched in 1998. Then, in 2001, AOL came out with their AIM messenger software for non-subscribers. There were also many smaller companies coming out with innovations. One instant message program I used back then was called ICQ (a pseudo-acronym created from the phrase "I See You").

At the time, ongoing news updates typically were found on a website's 'About' or 'News' page. Once these updates started to include more than straight-forward news, people began to refer to them as "weblogs". Open Diaries, launched in 1998, was an example of a website that began to host people's diaries online. It moved content past news and into updates on people's thoughts and feelings, as well their mentions of news items. LiveJournal was another popular service, launched back in 1999. The term "blog" was coined in 1999 when Peter Merholz, as a joke, broke apart the word 'weblog' on his weblog's sidebar into 'we blog'.

The Rise of Social Media Destinations

2001 is considered the year that the Internet "bubble" burst, and many Internet companies, who never had an understandable revenue model, began to go out of business. Well into the "burst" years, in 2003, Tom Anderson and Chris DeWolf began the service that became known as MySpace (a little trivia for you – the original name was SiteGeist and its original vision was as a web hosting company). Once launched as MySpace, first locally in southern California, its user focus was musicians, actors, and artists. When a competing site, Friendster, began expelling bands from their site for not complying with regulations, in addition to rumors that Friendster was going to become fee-based, MySpace experienced its meteoric rise in popularity and usage. MySpace was sold to News Corporation, still with no visible means of revenue, in 2005, for $580 million in cash.

Many of you have seen, or at least heard, about the movie "The Social Network," which was about the Facebook story. The first version of Facebook was launched in 2003 as a site called FaceMash. It originally was set up to compare two faces side-by-side, from various dormitory buildings at Harvard and select which photo was more "hot" than the other. At the time, Mark Zuckerberg filled his new project with photos by hacking into the Harvard school's computer security system and basically stealing the photo IDs that the dormitories used. There was no directory of students by photo in existence at the time, so when he launched FaceMash, people were interested in seeing the photos. Based on the popularity of this project, code began to be written for a new project called "thefacebook." Its original intent was to make the Harvard student directory which hadn't yet existed, with photos and basic information. Controversy ensued, not because Mark hacked into the university system, but because at the same time he was writing code for "thefacebook" he was also being paid to write code for three other students on campus for a project called "ConnectU," that would connect Harvard students. Zuckerberg might disagree (and his lawyers certainly did) but the three students, twins Cameron and Tyler Winklevoss and Divya Narendra, claimed Zuckerberg took their idea and used it as the basis for what became Facebook. Eventually, these three guys settled a lawsuit out of court with Mark Zuckerberg and Facebook in 2008 for a reported $65 million dollars.

With Facebook mostly focused on college students, MySpace remained the number one social networking site throughout 2007 and into early 2008. Facebook began to broaden its base of users and on April 19, 2008, Facebook beat out MySpace for the first time in the Alexa rankings (Alexa, now a subsidiary of Amazon.com, is considered a leading source for website rankings). MySpace began its continuous decline from that point forward. Why could MySpace not maintain its market position? There are only theories, but some say MySpace, unlike Facebook, was not innovating new features. Others have suggested that an advertising deal with Google so overloaded the site with advertisements that the site was too slow and unresponsive to use compared to Facebook. Whatever the reasons, MySpace faded into the background as Facebook rose to prominence.

Twitter was launched in July of 2006. I had an art friend who was an early Twitter adapter. She would post these really short phrases on her website that said where she was: "Now I'm at the store." "Now I'm at the bookstore." "Now I'm sitting watching TV." And I thought – really?? You are going to tell me where you are all day long on your website with your Twitter feed? I was really turned off and missed the whole point of Twitter in the early days.

Much like blogs grew out of online diaries, Twitter positioned itself not like Facebook but as a "microblogging" social network. Twitter rose to prominence right around the same time as Facebook, in the 2008-2009 time frame. Twitter allowed users to post an update but no longer than 140 characters, including spaces and punctuation. It became important to distill your thoughts. Or submit a lot of posts to complete a single thought. Some people have taken that approach. I think sometimes Twitter comes out of the social phenomenon of shorter attention spans. They figured users could handle one 140-character thought rather than a whole diary-like posting on a topic. What we used to refer to as the TV generation has definitely become the Twitter generation.

Many people are confused and ask what is the difference between Twitter and Facebook. I think of these as very different platforms with unique functions. Facebook is really attractive to people wanting to connect with friends and family they know, making new friends, posting photos and videos to share. Facebook is about connecting with your circle of "friends," even if your definition has evolved to include lots of people on your friends list that you do not know personally. Twitter, on the other hand, is more like an open ticker tape of people's postings. One feed goes out to everyone, and anyone can follow any other person they want in the feed (unless they are blocked). There is no need for approval as a follower. Twitter postings reach a wider audience. The search engine part of Twitter uses a concept referred to as the "hashtag." You can search on a hashtag and see all the postings made using that tag. No one has exclusive rights to hashtags. Some hashtags are used by a lot of people and end up on the "trending" list of popular hashtags. This list is constantly changing and updating. You are able to see posts with those hashtags even if you are not following those people. An example of a hashtag might be "#romance." You can search on that hashtag and see what everyone is posting that includes that hashtag. There is a list in the left screen column that shows the trending or popular hashtags. There is also more of an emphasis on Twitter with linking out to other sites (probably because of the limitation of 140 characters) and I find so many new and interesting resources, blogs, and cool stuff through what people link to. So I think of Twitter as a more public, open environment where I can search on hashtag topics, see a stream of quick updates from people I choose to follow and when I post, I know it's available publicly, not just to my list of followers.

There are Facebook lovers who just don't get Twitter and Twitter lovers who can't stand Facebook. But both have a place. Sometimes I am in my Facebook phase and post a lot there (facebook.com/KTMObooks) but more frequently, I am in my Twitter phase and more often post there (twitter.com/KTMObooks). Sometimes I do more reading of posts on Facebook and sometimes more on Twitter. You see, it's a mood thing. And it will all change when the next new shiny thing comes along.

LinkedIn is a networking site that was made specifically for professional people and their work life. It was actually launched at the same time as MySpace, back in 2003. Unlike the other social media sites, LinkedIn was cash-flow positive within 3 years because of its premium fee-based service. It removed some of the "noise" of more personal social sites like Facebook and Twitter, and has been a great resource for making and maintaining professional connections, finding job opportunities and participating in groups that have a strong professional work focus.

New Kids on the Block

Pinterest is a new kid on the block, launched in 2010. It allows people to bookmark (or "pin") images and categorize their collection of images into category "boards." Other users can share your "pins" by re-pinning them into their boards. Users can follow other user's boards of similar interests and see what they add. By January of 2012, it was reported that Pinterest had 11.7 million unique users. The site moved out of invitation-only status in August 2012, becoming open to everyone. It has been said that in 2012, Pinterest has seen an 866% increase in visitors, but that number might be due to it moving out of invitation-only mode. On the other hand, Pinterest could well be a top site in popularity in no time at all. Time will tell.

Instagram is a photo sharing service that allows users to alter and put interesting filters on their photos, add tags to them, and then post their altered photos on various social networks, to show what a fun photo they made. It is another site on a meteoric rise, though it is no longer an independent site. It was launched in October of 2010. It is said to currently have 100 million registered users and Facebook purchased the company for $1 billion dollars in April of 2012. Now there are some lucky founders for 2 years worth of work, but I digress. It is an "app" that is currently supported on smartphones, like the iPhone and

Android mobile phones. Instagram is the darling of the younger generation, with 50 % of the users falling in the age bracket of 18-34.

I like what one person said online, as he summed up his impression of popular social media websites: "Facebook is huge, Twitter is busy, Pinterest has a lot of women users, and Instagram is mostly young people." It almost sounds like a jingle.

Smaller Players on the Scene

While I will go into some depth on how scams operate on the major social media websites, there are many minor services out there which make up the social media landscape, but do not hold a large portion of the marketplace. If you are a user on one of these services, you need to be diligent about protecting yourself against scams on those sites as well. Scammers will go anywhere they think they can find victims. Anywhere. Trust me.

What's on the Horizon?

If we've learned anything in the history of the Internet, it is a fickled thing. Sites rise and become wildly popular only to be eclipsed by a new service and fade into the background. MySpace was the poster child for this phenomenon. Six months from now the picture of who is in and who is not may completely change from today's list of top sites. There will always be new things on the horizon. That's actually good news. Innovation and new sites lead to progress and improved services.

Scam Alert Red Flag

Look for the Scam Alert Red Flags throughout the book. These are important clues that will assist you in quickly recognizing when you are looking at a scam, BEFORE you give up information or money. This is the key to reducing the success rate of any given scam.

CHAPTER 2
FACEBOOK SCAMS

www.facebook.com

In today's social media landscape, Facebook is king of the hill, with a reported 750 million estimated unique monthly visitors recorded in September 2012. Right now, Facebook is clearly the largest social media destination website. And being the largest destination for social gatherings of people online means it is also a top focus for scammers looking to find fresh new victims and their cash.

Sometimes people get so into their postings and conversations with their friends, that they forget they are on a public website and they trust that those writing to them are actually trust-worthy people using Facebook. This is not always the case. Educating yourself on the common scams that can be found on Facebook will definitely help you use it with more confidence while not falling victim to the scammers. Familiarize yourself with these and be prepared.

1. Fake Facebook Notification Emails

These notifications will come to your email box and look like legitimate official Facebook emails, telling you that you have a new friend, someone posted a photo of you, or tagged you on a photo. You will want to click on the link in the email to see who has requested to be friends, or more compelling, who posted a photo of you. But once you click on that link, the trouble begins. The link may begin to install software on your computer, called spyware, which keeps track of your keystrokes seeking out passwords to your accounts. Or clicking on the link may install "worm" software and use your computer as a "slave" computer – launching cyber attacks from your computer, all without you even knowing it. The link could download a virus that will render your computer useless. Or the link could redirect you to a web page that looks exactly like Facebook (but it will be bogus). Once redirected to a new webpage, you will likely be asked to log in again, thus collecting your Facebook login information. Now the scammer can go into your Facebook account and send spam to other users, spreading the scam even further.

Some of these emails are more scary in tone. They may say that a friend has reported you to Facebook for a violation of their terms, instruct you to click on the link in order to review the report. Of course, any normal person is going to want to click on that link to see why they were reported. But it's a scam.

You may ask yourself, "What do scammers get out of this?" They do not appear to get money out of this particular scam, but they also have a desperate need for other people's "bandwidth" and account access, in order to send out hundreds of thousands of their emails or messages. Those messages may be targeting other people to steal their money. Scammers also need to send emails or messages out in a stealth mode, in a way it can not be traced back to them. Therefore, scammers are ultimately after two things: money and using other people's accounts to send out their scam messages.

2. Fake Facebook Status Posts

Facebook is a perfect platform for scammers. They can set up a fake profile and "personality" in an account relatively easily. They can then begin posting status updates with links attached that trick people into clicking on them. Of course, these fake profiles have to build up a healthy list of friends first, but once scammers do that, often their status updates get shared to other people's walls and then spread like wildfire. Fake status update postings fall into a few main categories:

1. A news story that compels you to click on the link.

An example of this would be some recent trending news story with a teaser that there is something important behind the scenes of this story that you'll want to know. Here is an example that spread quickly across Facebook:

```
I am part of the 99% of people who will
never drink Coca-Cola again after seeing
this video ->
```

The attached link went to a url: truthaboutcoke.us. The purpose of the bogus website page was to eventually redirect you to a survey to collect information from you which would include your Facebook login and other information which you should not be giving out to strangers. Here's another example:

```
McDonald's might be shut down because of
this. Click here to see why ->
```

Many of these scam postings leverage news items with a made-up twist to get you to click on the photo or the link in the posting. It's human nature to want to click, but you must refrain.

2. An OMG (Oh My God) status posting with a link.

```
OMG!! Guys, you have to see this: This
mother went to jail for taking this pic of
her son ->
```

Once you click on the above link, it first uses software to automatically share the same post with all your Facebook friends and then takes you to a survey to try and collect as much personal, login, and financial information as possible. Here's another tricky one, and hard to resist clicking on this link, especially when you think someone you know on

Facebook is posting it to you:

```
OMG! I can't believe you in this photo! >
```

or

```
LOL! You're famous now! [link]
```

3. Fake Facebook Identities

Can you tell whether a Facebook profile is fake or not? Not really. You can look at some indicators but there is no way to know for sure. I came across this problem when I ran a paid Facebook advertising campaign to promote my new author page. I began to see a pattern of people "liking" my page but when I checked their profiles, they had nothing posted to their own walls, few to no photos and yet had liked thousands of Facebook pages. Their bio information was spotty, at best. I am not saying all these profiles are fake, I am just saying it struck me as very odd. In August 2012, Facebook - in its 10-Q filing, admitted 83 million profiles out of a total of 955 million are bogus accounts. 83 million, wow. One person online compared that number to the size of Egypt's population.

And it's not only the scammers making this trouble. There have been reports of corporate companies creating fake identities to spread bad rumors about competitors or to make their own company look better. Police have created fake identities on Facebook in order to catch criminals and predators. Also, people who just can't disclose their identity (computer security professionals, high-visibility professionals, for example) create fake profiles on Facebook. Kids create fake profiles so they can accrue more points in the games popular on Facebook. And some people do it just for the fun of it. Okay, so that's settled. Fake profiles are pretty rampant on Facebook.

So we are back to asking ourselves, "How can you tell if a Facebook profile is fake?" Again, there is no sure-fire way. You have to look at the totality of the profile. Did they recently join and yet they have a high number on their friends list? Where do they say they are from, and does their friends list reflect a lot of people local to them or is it just spread out all over the world? Do they update their status and interact with people? If they do interact with people, does their story and tone of writing make sense (one fake profile was pretending to be a teenager but began referencing historical news events a teenager wouldn't typically be aware of. It wasn't the smoking gun but raised flags). Does the profile photo seem like it was taken from a model's website or some other site? Does their profile description say "Accept me to Farmville?" (and then look at everything else and see if you sense this is not a real identity). If they do put anything in their status updates, does anyone ever comment back on them?

There is also the practice of "profile cloning," where scammers steal the profile images from someone's account, use their basic information and then begin sending requests to all their friends. Scammers will get friended back because the profile looks like a person they know, even though it is a cloned account. In some cases, fraudsters will steal the information from other social networks. This works particularly well if it is a social media website the user doesn't typically use. This will help the cloned account be a little more difficult to notice at first. The scammers will use these cloned accounts to make more cloned accounts and eventually begin perpetrating message status scams with links to redirect users to bogus websites. And related to this, some scammers will create cloned accounts and then join groups or write to friends of friends and ask for money. The victim may not know the person personally (who is actually a cloned account), but sees they have many mutual friends of whom they do trust. This is also known as "affinity fraud."

There was one recent case in the news where a single woman had fabricated online personalities for two brothers and a younger cousin, all of whom had leukemia. Their facebook pages had hundreds of friends and many followers and well-wishers as these three family members battled cancer. They had twitter pages, updates, had skype chats (conveniently the camera was always broken) and it was reported that several women believed they were the girlfriend of one or other of the brothers. But it was all made up. A remarkable thing about this scam was that there were posts from these fake personalities dating back to 2009. Three years of completely virtual non-real people interacting with real people on social media. The woman, when finally caught, was not arrested because she had not gone after anyone's money. I'm not sure why she did it – for the sympathy? For the sport of it? It made me wonder how many people on my Facebook friends list are fake.

While there are lots of reasons a profile may be fake, I am going to just focus on the internet scammer – those who ultimately hope to get money out of victims, or information that eventually leads to money.

I had a fake person join my Facebook page, with probably a fake photo, and then they proceeded to post a message about how she and her daughter were being kicked out of their apartment and they just needed $500 wired to them to avoid eviction. This ballsy scammer with a fake profile joined my Facebook page - about scams, and proceeded to post their scam message to those who have 'liked' my scam page! Gotta love their nerve.

When fake profile scammers are seeking victims, here are the most scams they employ:

Money Fraud

Here is where a scammer will just ask for money outright. It may come as a "stranded" type of message ("I'm stranded in Europe and need you to wire me money"), or it may come as someone who is pretending to be a friend of a friend and asking for money. Or sometimes, it is a sad sob story about losing their house or having a terrible medical emergency and asking for money to help them out. Those who have generous hearts and like to help people in need may be the most susceptible to this scam.

Check Cashing Fraud

This is the classic scam where a scammer will develop some story as to why they are sending you a check. It may be they are pretending to buy something from you which you are mentioning or promoting on Facebook. My artist friends run across this all the time – some scammer pretending to want to buy one of their paintings. But it really happens to anyone offering anything for sale. Once you accept to receive a check from a scammer, they will have some story as to why the check they are sending is for more than the amount, by a lot. They may mention some non-existent third-party shipping company in their story and ask you to forward the difference to them via wire transfer. Or they might say their wife, secretary, or assistant made a mistake and please just wire the difference back to them. The catch? The original check will turn out to be counterfeit but your forwarded money is good. That is how this scam works.

Information "Phishing" Fraud

This scam is called phishing (pronounced "fishing") because the scammers set up fake web pages and lead people to the pages with fake posts or fake advertisements and then, like fishing, wait for victims to take the bait.

In phishing fraud, the goal of the scammer is to get you to give up your important information voluntarily – but deceitfully - because you'll think you are at a perfectly legitimate website looking at a perfectly legitimate form to fill out, but it is bogus. The website has been made by the scammer to look realistic so that they collect your login information, your bank account information, your credit card information or anything else you'll provide. Sometimes scammers fake login pages (including Facebook's own login page), or sometimes they create fake Facebook survey pages.

Why are they trying to collect your information? Scammers can do a lot of things with that information. They can use your credit card numbers. They can use the information to contact your bank and sometimes are able to convince your bank to add an email or the option of online banking to your accounts, giving the scammer full access your money. They can sell the information. They can use the information to open lines of credit. Believe me, they can do a lot with your information, so don't give it up in the first place.

4. Hijacked Facebook Accounts

Different than fake Facebook profiles, scammers will also hack into legitimate Facebook accounts in order to send out scam messages to all the friends on that person's account, which spread to other people's Facebook 'walls'. These messages will often have a link, with the goal to trick more people into clicking on the link. Clicking on the link will lead to either a virus getting downloaded to your computer or will lead you to a bogus website that will attempt to collect your login and other important information such as your bank account, social security number, or credit card number.

At first, people weren't sure if these messages were really from their friends. After we all saw enough examples of these fake messages on Facebook, it became a little easier for many people to spot them as fake. But sometimes the only way a person knows their Facebook account has been hacked is when their friends contact them saying there is a weird message posted on their wall. All you can do at this point is go into your Facebook account, change your password to something a bit harder to guess, and delete all these posted messages.

5. Fake Facebook Apps & Scripts

Facebook has a lot of third-party applications that are very useful for users. I use one on my own author page. But, of course, scammers are going to muck it all up by also developing fake 'apps' and trying to trick people into installing them. Usually the successful fake apps are the entertainment or gaming ones. The most famous fake app is the one which claims you can see who unfriended you on Facebook. Hundreds of thousands of people fall for that one. Another example is one which shows you your name in Chinese characters and allows you to post that to your wall. Fake.

6. Fake Facebook "Friend" Emails

Scammers will create emails, outside of Facebook, and make them look like they are official Facebook emails, typically saying someone has requested to be your friend, and asks you to click on the link to approve or ignore the request. When you click on the link, you will find the URL is not the official Facebook pathway but the page you land on will look exactly like a Facebook login page. That's the first piece of information they will steal from you. Your login information. Then a survey will present itself – distracting you from the fact the rest of this fake

Facebook page really doesn't reflect your account information. Scammers will collect all kinds of other information in the survey, if you fill it out.

Sometimes these fake emails appear to be coming from your friend (and their name on the email is exactly how they have it on Facebook, even if they use a middle name when they don't in the regular email) and the subject line will say something like, "For Kathleen" (it will have whatever your first name is). You then notice that the email address of your friend is not theirs but some random Yahoo email address. Your email address is correct but theirs is not. And their name and your name are correct. Inside the email, there is nothing but one link and it is one link you do NOT want to click on. It took me forever to chase down why this was happening to me. I changed my Facebook password. I had my friends who were on these emails change their password. I had a friend on these emails who did have a Yahoo account and I had her change her password. And I kept getting them. I scanned my computer to see if I had any spyware or keylogging malware software that has been installed and maybe was tracking my keystrokes. Nothing. And the spam emails kept coming.

Finally, I found an article online where, after many denials, Facebook admitted that a security hole in their system had been exploited by a hacker who was somehow collecting information via an advertising campaign. So while Facebook said they had fixed the hole, it was possible that spammers would continue to use the information they had already collected to continue to send spam emails. I still get one here and there, but for me, the frequency of receiving them has pretty much gone away. Scammers look for weaknesses in systems and then exploit them. That's what they are good at.

7. Fake Facebook Fee Threats

This one seems pretty far out there, but people fall for this one all the time, so it is worth a mention. Users will receive emails that basically say: Facebook has moved to a fee-based service, the user is overdue, and their access to Facebook will be suspended if they do not pay a fee within a certain (short) period of time. Should the user click on the link, they will be redirected to a bogus website where there will be instructions on how to wire the money to restore your account (of course, using a wire transfer service is how scammers keep themselves untraceable once they've stolen your money). And while they've got the user on the bogus website, there will also either be a login page or a survey to fill out. The scammer will attempt to collect as much information as possible – not only stealing your money, but your identity as well. And if they get your bank account number, they can take even larger sums of money from you.

Facebook is a free service to access and their revenue is generated from advertising. Should that change in the future, there would be a million news articles on it, so always google the issue before sending money to anyone, and see what has been posted online. Or go to the Facebook customer service link and write to them directly. Never wire money to someone you don't know.

8. Instagram Scams

I wanted to give Instagram its own chapter, but it is owned by Facebook and relatively new as a service so I'll cover it here. Instagram is a mobile phone 'app' that lets you place fun filters and layers and effects on your photos and then post them to your other social media websites. I have a lot of friends who use Instagram and I see many people posting Instagram photos to Facebook and Twitter. Facebook claims, as of September 2012, to have passed 100 million users.

People can comment on and "like" photos on the Instagram app much like other social media websites. So scammers are going to pull their usual tricks within the comments section of people's accounts, much like how scammers exploit the comment functionality on

Facebook. The other way we can talk about Instagram scams is how scammers use the photos on other social media websites to trick people.

On the photo community for Instagram, spam accounts with "get more followers" in their name are starting to infiltrate the network. They're easy to spot as they usually have no photos on their profile pages, and promise links that will give you "25,000 followers."

The ellipsis button on each photo lets you report inappropriate photos, with a flagging function on the top right arrow of each profile.

But who's got the time and energy to report the dozens of scam profiles cropping up each day? Just be aware and think twice before clicking on any links or suspicious photos.

CHAPTER 3
YOUTUBE SCAMS

www.youtube.com

YouTube is a video sharing website created by three former PayPal employees back in 2005. It has become famous for personal videos of people doing all sorts of things that go "viral" (meaning without any promotional effort, suddenly hundreds of thousands of people are viewing the video just by word of mouth). YouTube is no longer an independent company, with Google having purchased the company in November of 2006 for $1.65 billion (that's billion) dollars. Now, YouTube operates as a subsidiary of Google. It is ranked number 2 for social media destination sites, though the thing that is social about it is not back and forth chit-chat, but the sharing of personal and professional videos. Let's look at the types of scams you might run across on YouTube:

1. YouTube Comment Scams

Scams are perpetrated through the comments section of videos. Some are out-right spams for Viagra or Cialis ads, other scam comments will target certain videos and make claims about those videos that are not true. Or they will target technical how-to videos and claim they have a secret shortcut fix in the comments and provide a link. But the link just goes to a fake phishing website which tries to collect your personal information and your login passwords.

Other times, the scams sound urgent or threatening. One scammer was leaving messages in the comments area of a lot of different videos – pretending he was from the YouTube support staff, saying that the user's account would be shut down unless they sent their password to this support guy by a certain date. Of course, YouTube would never do this and this scammer was just collecting people's passwords. Why? So he could get into the account and post his deceitful videos but more likely, the scammer would try that same password in other accounts, because people do not use lots of different passwords. There could be some small chance the same password would work in the person's PayPal account and then the scammer would have access to money.

There is also the scam on YouTube which are the fake

comments. There might be a video of a particular product and then a bunch of comments underneath saying how great the product is, but those comments were placed there by fake posters, or people from that product company pretending to not be from that company.

2. YouTube Content Scams

One thing to keep in mind with YouTube is that anyone can post anything and thus there is no way to know if the content of a video is the truth or not. That is a big thing on YouTube. A lot of the videos related to products or the latest how-to-make-a million-dollars schemes or videos on how to win the lottery – some are set up so they look like news reports but they are really just commercials. Others are set up to look like instructional videos on how to get in on and invest in pre-IPO technology stocks. All scams. There is just a lot of misinformation out there and you need to have a critical mind and double check things through other sources.

3. YouTube Notification Emails

This scam includes the classic phishing emails that look as if the email is coming from YouTube, have the

YouTube logo, and general look and feel. The email will be notifying you that a video you uploaded has been approved, a video you've been tagged in has been approved, or just that YouTube has a message waiting for you. The email will then have a link for you to click on. If you hover your mouse over the link and do NOT click on it, you will see the actual destination of the link is definitely not YouTube. But someone not paying attention will click on that link and land on a page that has been made to look exactly like a YouTube page. It is not. There they will try and get you to log in (and thus get your password) and likely you'll be presented with a "survey" that will look like it's coming from YouTube. Scammers try to collect as much personal information as they can – your bank account, your social security number – whatever they can get.

Other tricky stories scammers use to get you to click on a link in the email:

> - you need to provide your cellphone number before viewing a video (and then you'll start to get a bunch of spam messages sent to your cellphone, or worse, a new monthly charge)

> - the email will say your version of Adobe Flash is outdated and needs to be updated before viewing YouTube videos (and clicking that link will actually begin the download of a virus to your computer)

- the email will actually look like it is coming as a Facebook notification and will say a video of you has been posted on YouTube

- the email will claim someone has lodged a complaint against a video you have uploaded to YouTube and the link will be so you can view the complaint (but it really goes to a fake page to collect your login and other important information on a form there that looks like it from YouTube

4. YouTube Typo Scam Sites

These are domains purchased by scammers to trap people into going to their bogus website because they mis-typed the name they meant to go to. If you put in YouTub.com by mistake, you will likely land on one of these sites. Some have been set up to look like YouTube (if they look just like YouTube but don't actually say the name of YouTube, they are not doing anything illegal). Other sites don't even pretend to look like YouTube but hope when you land there, they can get you to fill out information, enter a drawing, win a prize, or any story they can come up with to get your information.

5. Tips to Stay Safe on YouTube

- When you receive an email looking like it's from YouTube, regardless of what the message is, do NOT click on the link in the email. Just manually go to the site yourself in a new browser window and log into your account manually and see if there are any messages there for you.

- Be careful when you first go to YouTube that you are typing the url in correctly and do not end up on some scammer site with a slight variation of the real name. For example, "premium-youtube.com" is NOT the same as youtube.com. Don't be fooled.

- Just because a video is on YouTube, it does not mean the content of the video is true. Don't always believe what you see. Some videos are intentionally false. Never believe a product recommendation based upon a YouTube video. Get more input from many difference sources before coming to a decision. And no, that cat really didn't drive that car in that video.

- YouTube is an open forum for the sharing of videos. That means there will be shocking and explicit videos there. Monitor what your children are seeing and monitor what they are uploading. Children don't always understand the impact of uploading photos and videos to the Internet. They think this is no big deal but we, as adults, know nothing ever goes away. Children can have a false sense of security and privacy and this can be very dangerous. Likewise, monitor any communications minors may be having with someone in email as a result of a video they have uploaded.

SCAM TIP:

There is NO legitimate reason for someone giving you money to ask you to wire money back to them or to someone else.

CHAPTER 4
EBAY SCAMS

www.ebay.com

With over 210 million estimated unique monthly visitors recorded in September 2012, eBay is ranked number 3 for social media destination sites. The site is actually an auction and selling platform, with lots of active forums and message boards for community interaction. Because of the large amount of anonymous transactions taking place on eBay, with buyers and sellers who may not have any established reputation, scammers have flocked to the site in droves to find ways to take money from victims. Here are some of the more common scams on eBay:

1. Phishing Email Scam

Scammers send out emails that mimic the look and feel of eBay, so you think you are getting an official email from eBay. But it is not. This happens with all the major sites.

Scammers can fake email headers so the FROM address also may look like it is from eBay. But the REPLY-TO address will be different (because they may want to receive replies to the email from potential victims), and typically be a disposable email account at a service like Gmail, Hotmail, Live.com, Yahoo, etc.

These bogus emails will typically include a link that looks legitimate. But if you place your mouse cursor over the link (do NOT click on it), you will see in your lower link status bar what the real link destination is and it is often very different.

If the goal of the scammer is to get you to click on the link and go to their own web page, they will typically have designed that page to make it look like a real eBay page. That is so people not paying close attention may click and still think everything they are doing is okay and they are still at eBay's website. But they are not.

Typically, at this point, the goal is to get as much information as possible – your eBay password, even your PayPal login or your banking account. Whatever they can trick you into providing to them. Their fake site will collect whatever fields you have filled in and add it to their database for later use. If they get your eBay login, they can use your account to set up fake auction listings and trick other people out of their money using your good eBay reputation. But we'll talk about that more in a bit.

Related to this idea of a fake web page, scammers will set up a fake page that looks like an eBay auction listing page. But it is fake. Then the scammer will go on eBay and write to a number of sellers and ask them if their item is similar to "this one" and then link to the fake page. When the seller arrives at the fake page to look, it asks them to log in (and eBay often does this to validate your access). If the seller logs in, then the scammer has their account login information.

If any of this has happened to you, change your account passwords immediately and get help from eBay to remove any listings that may have been listed on your account by the scammer.

2. Second Chance Offers

At one point, eBay implemented a feature called "Second Chance Offers." The idea of the feature was to allow the seller the ability, if they were not able to complete the sale with the winning bidder (or they had duplicate items for sale), they could send a Second Chance Offer to any of the other persons who had a bid on the item. So this opened an opportunity for scammers to exploit. Scammers would seek out high-ticket sold items on eBay and create a fake email that looked like a Second Chance Offer. They would send it to all the under-bidders. They never had the item but the unsuspecting victims did not know that. If one or more of the under-bidders responded to the fake email, the scammer would launch into a story about how was better the sale occur outside of eBay. They would have all different kinds of reasons why but it came down to trying to convince the victim to make the deal outside of eBay. This problem continues today.

One way to combat this problem is write directly to the seller, through the eBay system, to confirm they really have sent you a Second Chance Offer. This won't be helpful if the scammer has hacked into the person's account. But in most cases, the scammers have not hacked the account – they are just sending these faked emails from a disposable Yahoo, Gmail, Live.com or Hotmail account. There are so many faked Second Chance Offer emails that many buyers just ignore them all and do not respond to any Second Chance Offers from sellers. Also, it is always advisable not to take your eBay transactions outside the eBay system.

3. Hijacked Accounts

Hijacked accounts on eBay are an insidious problem and slowly destroy the trust a buyer needs to feel to use the site. Is a seller for real or not? Can I trust this seller not to rip me off? These are tough questions. But they become even tougher when scammers take sellers who have a great track record with customers and hack into their account and begin listing items under their name – items that don't exist. Now, of course, the hackers have to do a few additional things to get your money. They have to find a way for any emails you send or notifications from eBay on the fake listings to not be sent to the actual owner of the account they have hijacked. Sometimes they just try to work fast enough that they are done before the owner of that seller's account can change the password again. Other times, the scammer will attempt to change the email that is on file for that account. The scammer will also have to convince the buyer to pay them via wire transfer. That way, once the victim's money is picked up by the scammer, they are untraceable and the money is gone. **You'll do yourself a favor by just refusing to use wire transfers for *any* transactions you do online.** And be, at least, suspicious if a seller sells costume jewelry and suddenly has a bunch of listings for high-end electronics. It's at least worth a second look why that is so.

Scammers also hack into accounts to collect the names and email addresses of recent buyers.

If your account has been hijacked or you suspect another account has been hijacked, report it immediately: http://pages.ebay.com/help/account/securing-account.html

4. Overpayments

I see a version of this scam strategy everywhere online. It is typically referred to as the "Overpayment Scam" or the "Fake Buyer Scam." At some time or another, anyone selling anything online has dealt with this scam. What the scammer does is pretend they want to buy your item. They don't really care what your item is because their goal is not the item but the cash they are going to get from you. So they don't need to provide a valid shipping address. They will have some story about why they need to pay with a money order or cashier's check. When you receive the check, it turns out to be for far more than the amount, with a request to wire the remainder of the money to someone else (or they claim they made a mistake and ask the difference be wired back to them). If the seller falls for this scam, they send out the item and wire the difference in money to the "buyer" (i.e. scammer), only to find out the original check was counterfeit. Now the seller is out the item and the cash, often ranging from $1500 to $5000. If a scammer claims to have used a US Postal money order, sellers can confirm its authenticity by calling the USPS Postal Inspector's Money Order Verification System at 1-866-459-7822.

If a scammer offers to pay by credit card, it will turn out later that the card was stolen even if it clears at first. The seller will eventually experience a charge-back and be out the money. If a scammer agrees to pay with PayPal, they will often try and send a faked email that looks like a PayPal 'payment received' confirmation email, hoping the seller never actually checks their PayPal account themselves, until it is too late. Scammers want to rush sellers through this scam because the more time passes, the higher the chance the potential victim, the seller, will figure out something is wrong.

5. Empty or Junk Package

This is when a buyer buys something on eBay, and the package arrives but the box is either empty or contains a cheap imitation of the real thing purchased.

This also happens in reverse – a buyer receives the package, replaces the good item with an item of lesser value and then claims the item is "not as described." In almost all cases, eBay will give the buyer their money back. They can take the more valuable item and resell it. The seller is the loser in this case.

This switch-a-roo often happens in the collectibles category where the buyer will switch a valued collectible item with one that is of lesser value and then attempt to return the package to the seller and get a refund. They often get away with it, so sellers often place a mark on the item that can only be seen under black light. That mark has to be confirmed before the seller will refund the money. This helps reduce the problem a bit.

Sometimes, the recourse for this entire category of scams is difficult. Some suggestions: As a buyer, it helps to use PayPal and pay with a credit card so if PayPal won't help you, you can turn to your credit card company. As a seller, before closing the box, take a photo of the item in the box, with something in the photo showing the shipping label. Ship the item according to the eBay and PayPal guidelines so you can get help if something goes wrong. Still, this is a difficult thing for sellers, because in most cases eBay sides with the buyer.

6. Partial Refund

This buyer scam is when the buyer claims the item

they've purchased is not what they were expecting and they are unhappy. Rather than ask for a full refund, they ask for a partial refund. They are hoping that the seller – wanting to please their customer and maintain their good feedback rating, will provide the partial refund. One way for sellers to lessen the impact of this type of practice is to just have a policy of no partial refunds, only full refunds when the item is returned.

7. Shill Bidding

This scam has existed from the very first days of eBay and, all these years later, continues to be an on-going problem, basically because it is difficult to identify and prove.

In shill bidding, a seller will list an item for sale and then through one or more other accounts, established under other identities or perhaps even other family members, submit bids on that item. The goal may be to raise the price and/or to keep the item from selling at a lower price than they want. Sometimes the goal is to get several bids on an item and thus improve the placement of the item in the search results. At other times, these shill bidders are after buying items at low prices and then giving themselves great feedback ratings in order to improve the overall feedback and selling "reputation." If, at the end of an auction, the shill bidder is the high bidder, the seller and the "buyer" (which is just them under another account, or a family member) can agree to mutually retract the bid. It takes effort and planning but can be done.

While not always true, shill bidders are often new sellers. Sometimes you can notice a shill bidder because they often only bid on the items of one seller, which is not normal buyer activity. You might also notice that the bidder has a lot of retractions on their record.

If you feel you have run across a shill bidder, report it to Ebay and let them research it and make the final decision: http://pages.ebay.com/help/policies/questions/how-report-violation.html.

Shill bidding is actually an illegal activity and eBay may, in the proper circumstances, refer certain cases to the local law enforcement authorities.

8. Fakes Items

This is just an eBay version of a scam that is happening all over the Internet and, well, all over the world – counterfeit knock-off's being sold as the real thing. The number one category for counterfeit items is electronics, number two is shoes, followed by counterfeit prescription drugs, CDs/DVDs, clothing, perfume, watches, cigarettes, computer hardware, and toys & games. Not all these categories can be sold on eBay, but for those that can, you can bet there are counterfeit versions being sold on the site.

Some of the ways you can spot fake and counterfeit items on eBay:

- if the price is unbelievably good on a brand name item, it likely *is* unbelievable and counterfeit

- if the photo allows, examine to the best of your ability the quality of the product – imitations use cheaper, lighter materials and often the stitching is less than professional

- look carefully at the logos and brand markings – counterfeit logos are often slightly different, a larger or smaller font, a slight variation in the color, or the placement of the logo on the product

- compare the traditional packaging of the brand item with the packaging sold on eBay. While not always true, often the counterfeit items are sold with no packaging or "out of the box"

- if the brand product offers model or serial numbers, check those against manufacturer numbers – often counterfeits have numbers but they do not match what the manufacturer or brand uses

- a seller can't last long with a good feedback rating selling fake goods, so only deal with those sellers who have a long and high feedback ranking

- many counterfeit listings are private (only pre-approved bidders may view the listing) and often have inflated shipping costs

- many counterfeit listings have rush rush rush language in their listing and typically are only 1-3 day listings. This is to trick you into acting before you've given it proper thought

If you have been sold a counterfeit item that has been described in the listing as a brand product, you can report that to eBay: http://pages.ebay.com/help/policies/replica-counterfeit.html

9. Fake Escrow Account

Fake escrow account scams are prevalent on eBay (and Craigslist as well). An escrow account is an objective third-party company where payments for a high-priced item can be made and held until the item is received by the buyer. The seller knows the money has been paid to the escrow service and the buyer has a chance to make sure the condition of the item is what the seller says it is before having the escrow service release the money. Escrow accounts are a way to reduce the sense of risk on both sides of a transaction. How scammers exploit this is they will set up a fake escrow account under a name that sounds similar to a well-known escrow company name. So when the buyer pays the money to the escrow account, they are, in fact, paying it to the scammer who then disappears because they never had a high-priced item to sell. Or on the reverse side, when the scammer is the buyer, the buyer will show the payment has been made to an escrow account (which they set up to look like a real company) and you, as the seller, go ahead and ship the item only to find out you are not going to be paid because the escrow account was faked by the buyer. Buyer escrow scams happen because the scam buyer is trying to get something for free (as opposed to cash). Seller escrow accounts happen because the scam seller is trying to get cash and is less concerned about what item is being sold.

Escrow scams usually happen on expensive items - like cars, and as a seller you can avoid this by using only eBay-approved escrow services: escrow.com and iloxx.de. Also, only deal with people who have an established selling or buying reputation on their feedback scorecard. If you are a seller that did not get paid, file an Unpaid Item at http://pages.ebay.com/help/sell/unpaid-items.html . At least you will get back your listing fees, but your item will still be gone.

10. Pick-up Item

Proof that an item was received by the buyer is a tricky scam but one easily overcome. PayPal will only accept a shipping tracking number as proof, so if buyers arrange to pick up an item from you, there is no tracking number involved. That puts you, the seller, at more risk. How scammers exploit this is they pay by PayPal, show up and get the item, and then proceed to claim to eBay or PayPal that the item was never received. They get their money back. This is because even if you had photographic proof of the item being received, or a video recording of the event – all PayPal accepts for verification is a shipping tracking number. So here is how you protect yourself on this scam: when a transaction involves the buyer coming to pick up an item, ONLY deal in cash. No cashier's checks or money-orders – CASH. Problem solved.

11. Gift Cards

This scam is so popular that eBay has limited the number of gift cards a seller can list. How this scam works is simple: the scammer typically has shoplifted gift cards at a store, and then turns around and sells them on eBay. The problem for the buyer is the card is completely worthless unless it was purchased and paid for at the store (it is an inactive card and can not be activated if the scammer shoplifted it to begin with). But the buyer doesn't know that yet and proceeds to pay for the card. My advice is not to deal with any seller that offers a lot of gift cards. Only deal with sellers that have an established high feedback rating. And only pay using a credit card so you have some recourse there as well.

12. Stolen Credit Card Scam

Once users started getting smart to the counterfeit money order approach, many scammers switched to stolen credit card numbers. And you'd think that would not be a problem. If a credit card is stolen it won't pass the credit card company's authentication. But it does. That is because the scammers are exploiting a sweet spot for them – after the credit card number is stolen (typically online) but before it is reported as stolen, it still clears as good. But of course, once the owner or the credit card company realizes it is stolen, they will issue a charge-back and the seller is on the hook for the total amount. And the seller will have already shipped their item. Also, in most cases, scammers know the stolen credit card's number but do not know the billing address. So they often come up with some story about moving so, if pressed, they can say they are in the process of changing the billing address. Every time I have asked them to give me the current billing address on file for that card, the scammer disappears (because they know they can not proceed with the scam). So if they do give me an address, I can call the credit card company and ask them to confirm if that is the correct billing address.

13. Fake Drop-Shipper

This scam happens when a seller with a good reputation is approached by someone claiming to be a drop-shipper (or worse, just someone who needs help selling items). A drop-shipper is a business that stocks merchandise and sells it to you (the reseller) – but ships the merchandise directly to your customer. The items are typically things that would seem to sell easily. The drop-shipper offers if the eBay seller will list items for him, he will handle everything after the sale. All the eBay seller has to do is keep their agreed upon amount and forward the rest back to the drop-shipper so he can ship the items out to the customer. But the drop-shipper is a scammer. If the eBay seller hasn't done their homework, they don't find out they've been scammed until after an item sells and it turns out the drop-shipper has nothing to ship. The eBay seller is left holding the bag and will have to refund money to the customer. The selling reputation of the eBay seller is at risk and the eBay seller has also lost the cash he forwarded to the drop-shipper scammer. But this is an easy one to avoid – just don't ever agree to these shady type of relationships – let people open their own eBay account and do their own marketing.

14. Western Union Payment

As you know, I'm an advocate of getting all wire transfer services out of your life. Scammers NEED them because they are the most successful way they get cash from you and be completely untraceable. Just the simple act of refusing wire transfers would solve a lot of problems. But let's get back to this scam. In this scam, the scammer will offer to pay via Western Union (this is also done with PayPal, so it's not specific to Western Union) and then proceed to send the seller a fake email looking like a payment confirmation on the buyer's part. Sellers who don't double check this and just believe the email think the payment has been made, and they proceed to send the item. As a secondary insult, the scammer will send another email which looks like it comes from Western Union asking the seller to provide all kinds of information before their money is "released." Now the scammer has your item and your personal information which can be used for identity theft. If this scam was done with PayPal, they often then have your PayPal login information, if you gave that up.

This idea of sending faked payment confirmation emails is still a rampant practice. It targets sellers who don't take that extra minute or two to check their own account. Take that extra time. It's worth your online safety.

15. Fake Pre-Paid Shipping Account

In this scam, the buyer requests that the item be delivered using their pre-paid FedEx or UPS account number. They say they are having the package sent to a work or some other address. The seller sends out the package only to learn that the shipping account number did not belong to that buyer, leaving the seller on the hook. The way for the seller to protect themselves from this scam is always use their own shipping account, not an account belonging to someone else.

16. Send To My Friend Scam

You'll be able to recognize this scam because the buyer will be requesting their purchase be sent to a different address (their story will be a friend or relative), typically in some foreign country where your item is unlikely to be retrievable, like Russia or Belarus. The buyer will use an eBay and/or PayPal account that has been hacked into and when the fraud is discovered, the monies will be withdrawn from the seller's account. Then the seller is on the hook for the item, the shipping cost, as well as the listing and final fees. Scammers like to do this with high-ticket items and electronics. They like to get-in-get-out very quickly with this scam. This is also a popular scam around the holidays, when sellers are processing a higher volume of orders and legitimate buyers are making legitimate requests to send items to other addresses.

17. The Redirect Scam

In this scam, the seller is the scammer. The seller will have a listing and in the listing, they have made a page that looks like it has text and images, but the page description has been coded in such a way that it is one large image, but it looks like separate text and images. It is not. And that is a tricky thing because the whole image is clickable so anywhere you click on the description area, you will end up being redirected to the scammer's website. You can notice this if you pass your mouse over the description area without clicking on anything and see in the URL status bar towards the bottom of the screen the real destination link. But the scammer is counting on you not noticing and the truth is, most people do not notice. Once the user is at the seller's set-up bogus site, the page mimics the eBay login page and the user thinks they are just being asked to confirm their login. But then the scammer has their login and can proceed to post more listings like this to trick other people, or just post fake listings to steal other people's money.

A variation of this scam is when the seller posts a fake listing and puts a fake report listing button on their listing description. They then put an x-rated photo in their photo gallery, inciting users to report the listing. But if users click on the fake reporting button, they will be redirected to a fake login page and again – the scam seller gets their account login information.

When I'm not feeling confident of a listing that asks me to log in, I open a new browser window, type in "ebay.com," log in, and then find my way back to where I was, knowing I am already logged in.

18. Contact Me Scam

Here the scam seller will list an item, typically a high-priced item, and use the "pre-approved bidders" feature. This means only bidders that are pre-approved by the seller can bid on the item. So a buyer, liking the price and wanting to bid, contacts the seller to get pre-approved. It is at this point that the seller has some story to get the buyer to take the transaction off eBay. That is when you know it is a scam. Keep all your transactions within eBay to avoid scammers who need to deal with you outside the system in order to steal your cash.

19. Fake eBay Safe Payment Scam

This is related to the escrow scam already explained in Section 9 of this chapter, in that buyers who are running a scam will make up names for "safe buying" programs – and create fake websites. Sometimes thei fake names of these non-existent escrow accounts are targeted at sellers who just don't take the time to look, like "eBay Safe Purchase Program" (which doesn't exist). The buyer will claim to make their payment to that service until they receive the item. The seller will discover the Safe Payment program was all made up after the item is already gone. This scam works best when used on high-priced items because the scam buyer can then steal a high-ticket item from the seller.

20. The New Buyer/Seller Scam

Scammers will try and take advantage of creating a new eBay account and see how much damage they can do before they are shut down. Buyers and sellers alike know this and are wary of new profile accounts. But everyone was new on eBay at some point. Whether you are a buyer or a seller, be wary of doing business with brand new accounts with no feedback. As a seller, you can insist a new buyer have a verified PayPal account and that will provide a little reassurance. As a buyer, I'd just skip sellers that have no feedback record, or their feedback record was built upon buying a bunch of small-priced items.

21. Fake Ticket Scams

Fake tickets are as prevalent on eBay as they are on Craigslist. This scam tends to be more active around big events like the SuperBowl. Ticket buyers of a hot event tend to be more excited than smart and do not take the time to make sure the tickets are for real, under fear of losing the opportunity to get the tickets in the first place. The scammers are counting on that.

Red Flag Clues

- someone from Yugoslavia is not going to have SuperBowl tickets

- never pay for tickets online with a wire transfer. Just don't do it. Pay with a credit card. Use PayPal. Even better, use your credit card through PayPal

- Look over the seller's feedback and comments from others

22. Charity Auction Scam

There are many auctions on eBay that state that either all of the proceeds or a portion of the proceeds will be donated to a charity. The seller is hoping you will give a little more, because it is for charity. eBay has set rules for listings that are charity auctions. These rules have been put in place to try and reduce some of the intentional, as well as unintentional, fraud. All charity listings must go through MissionFish, which has its own set of rules and charges a fee for its service. Sellers that do not want to go through MissionFish can still do a charity auction but the seller's listing must include a scanned copy of the document in which that charity approved the auction. Here is where scammers – who make all types of counterfeit documents, have their loophole. They just make a fake scanned document. As a buyer, proceed with charity listings with caution and assume MissionFish auctions are a little safer.

23. Feedback Fraud

Scammers, whether they are buyers or sellers, want to boost their feedback rating before going after the high-priced items and then disappearing, only to set up a new account and start their scam all over again. So scammers will buy and sell items that cost one penny, often to each other, if a group of them are working together. They give each other great ratings. You can tell who is doing this by looking at their feedback score and taking a little additional time to click on a few of the items and get a sense of what was being sold or purchased. If it seems like they are relatively new and have a lot of penny transactions, you are probably looking at someone to stay away from.

Here are some tips for having a safer experience on eBay:

- Do your research. Know the product in which you are interested. Collect as much information on the product online as you can. Do not trust that just because a listing says it is authentic that it is. If it is a product that is known for having knock-off counterfeits, you can bet those will be present on eBay.

- Ebay has a system for contacting sellers through their system. It's there to keep you safer. Do not contact sellers through any email they list in their description area, even if they say that is the only way to contact them – or maybe *especially* if they say that.

- There are lots of good reasons to have a listing of short duration. Lots of legitimate sellers choose to do this because most views occur at the beginning and then again at the end of the time period. But scammers almost always use a short-duration listing because they need to get in and get out quickly before the fraud is discovered and reported. So be wary of short-duration listings, but use them as only one red flag in combination with other existing red flags.

- Most scammers are located in countries where the law can not or does not pursue them. So if you are dealing with anyone in a country of question, proceed with great care or just decide to not proceed at all. And if any buyer or seller says they are "temporarily out of the country", this is a classic line used by scammers wanting to trick you into wiring money to them. Match where the person says they are from and what format the money is in. A seller from New York should not have the bid currency converting to Euros.

- A scam seller isn't going to accept a return on their item or your money so their listing may make this great claim about their product and offer a money-back guarantee and cheap shipping. Don't blindly believe the claims made in a listing. They can promise what they want because they will steal your money and disappear.

- Don't be fooled by a large number in a seller's feedback rating. Take the time to look at the actual comments and check out the type of items they've sold in the past. But if a scammer has hacked into and stolen the use of someone's account, they will suddenly start listing items that are not like what the seller has been selling in the past – so look at the details over time. Also scammers tend to hack into accounts that haven't been used for awhile. Make sure there isn't a sudden location change or a sudden change of payment methods being accepted.

- Take time to examine the photos used in the listing. Do they look like the seller took these or are they from manufacturer stock photos? Does the background look like someone was trying to photograph the item on the shelf of a store? Does the photo look like it's been stolen from other listings on eBay?

- Reach out and contact the seller if that will make you feel more comfortable. Legitimate sellers are eager to make legitimate buyers comfortable.

- If a phone number is listed in the listing, look it up online and see if you can verify the location and possibly even the name associated with that phone number.

- If you are unable to contact a seller via the contact button and have given them reasonable time to respond, you have a valid reason to cancel your bid. It doesn't necessarily mean the seller is a scam artist, but it is still a good reason not to proceed.

- Scammers sometimes like to hide their listings in weird categories. If the listing you are interested in is located in a weird category, start doing more research to look for other clues to determine if it is a valid listing.

- We can never repeat this enough throughout this book, but NEVER use wire transfer services for your online dealings. Scammers need wire transfer services to easily steal money and disappear without a trace. So just refuse to use wire transfer services. If you are a buyer, best bet is to use your own credit card through PayPal and then you'll have two layers of protection – PayPal's policies and the protection of your credit card company.

- Avoid Second Chance Offers unless you know who you are dealing with.

- If there are links in a listing, roll your mouse over each of the links without clicking on them and see where their destination is pointing. If it is a shortened URL and you can not tell, do NOT click on it.

- eBay's login page (and PayPal's, too) actually begins with *https://* (to designate it is on a secure server). Fake scammer sites will just be *http://* (with no 's', so don't log into any fake eBay page that doesn't have the secure server designation).

Keep yourself educated on all the scams that go on with eBay. These scams can and probably will appear in various forms on all of the selling platforms available online. If they work on eBay, scammers will try them on every other selling website out there.

CHAPTER 5: TWITTER SCAMS

www.twitter.com

With an estimated 200 million unique monthly visitors recorded in September 2012, Twitter is ranked number 4 for social media destination sites. The site is known as a "micro-blogging" website and has both similarities to Facebook as well as unique differences. Users may be on Facebook and Twitter but will lean towards spending more time on one or the other. There are a number of scams to be on the lookout for when using Twitter:

1. Fake Twitters

There seem to be armies of people and businesses on Twitter building fake profiles – lots of them. Their goal is to create a Twitter experience where having a very large following will make your brand or company, or you as a person, seem important and popular. In the election year of 2012, it was discovered that contender Mitt Romney's Twitter account saw an increase of 21% followers in the month of July 2012. 23% of those accounts never sent a single "tweet" posting and 10% had already been removed by Twitter administration by the end of the month. I'm not saying their campaign did that intentionally, I am just saying it seemed to be filled with a lot of fake accounts. Some fake accounts will post positive (or negative) messages about a political candidate or a competing company. Scammers may automate messages in their many fake accounts to jump on to "trending" issues, for additional exposure. The reputation of Twitter is really on the line, but it will always be a cat-and-mouse game between Twitter trying to identify these fake accounts and shutting them down, and the scammers with their automated tools creating new fake accounts.

Can you know when a Twitter account is fake?

If they are good, the answer is not really, but here are some broad signs to look for. It's not any one or all of these clues, but I would say if a bunch of these fit, the odds of the account being fake are definitely higher.

- If the account is relatively new and within weeks they already have 25,000 followers, the chances the account is fake are much higher.

- If the account seems to link to advertising material or suspicious websites that seem unrelated to the person's interest areas, there is a chance it is a fake account.

- Lack of account setup- no photo (or fake photo), and no profile info is filled out – it is likely to be a fake account.

- Lots of followers but little to no tweets or tweeting no human person could do (like 50-100 a day, every day), it likely to be a fake account (or some real person has NO offline life!)

- Over 10,000 "followers" but no discernible connection to a real website nor can any other references to the profile's name be found in search engines.

- If an account has a slight misspelling of a celebrity's name, the odds are high the account is fake.

- If the account links to other accounts that also appear to be fake. Scammers create networks of fake accounts that all talk to each other in order to appear legitimate.

2. Instant Followers Scam

Companies and individual people "sell" followers. Let's look at the numbers to see why people are selling fake accounts: if you are a scammer who controls 20,000 fake accounts and you are selling "followers" to unsuspecting people wanting to build their following and the going rate is, say, around $20 per 1000 followers – and your fake followers can follow more than one customer – you can see how the potential money adds up quickly. And these scammers aren't working hard for their scam – they have software that pretty much automates much of the process of selling fake accounts.

Ever since I first began my author account on Twitter, I have had one or two accounts every day follow me and in their bio I would see the claim that they can get me thousands of followers instantly, for $59 or whatever. Usually the photo has been a scantily-clad woman, and if they have had tweets at all, it has been about how to get more followers. These are fake automated scam accounts, ready to take your money and then have their large network of fake accounts link to your Twitter account. These scammers can even set up fake accounts by keywords so they look like they are relevant to you. But there are no real people behind these accounts. I report every single one to Twitter as spam accounts.

Twitter is much more effective if you have 500 followers who really care about who you are and what you are about – who really do read your posts, than 35,000 followers who don't. Think about audience building on Twitter not as a numbers game, but as a quality game. In the long run, quality matters.

3. Twitter Apps Scam

There are many applications (apps) on Twitter, written by third-party companies, that make the Twitter experience more manageable and more enjoyable. Some of these help automate the management of followers and postings. Other applications help filter the feed so you can conduct real-time group "chats." But each time an app uses the data from the Twitter feed, the app user needs to sign into their twitter account and approve that application, typically by pressing an ALLOW button. Scammers exploit this process by posting Tweets that hide the link with a shortened URL (common on Twitter) and they then send you to a page to either collect your information or present you with a fake survey to win something in order to collect even deeper personal and financial information from you (they are most often in search of your login passwords, bank accounts, PayPal login, social security number).

One of these scams spread like wildfire last year. The post was "I have spent 11.6 hours on Twitter. How much have you? Find out here," and the link was shortened so you weren't sure where it went until you clicked on it. If you did and then clicked on the ALLOW button (which you would because you might be thinking this app is going to calculate the time you've spent on Twitter), it actually allowed a rogue scam app to post a message on your twitter feed that basically said the same thing and spread the message further. It was estimated that the link was clicked on 10,000 times before it was noticed and shut down. What was the goal? To get people to click on to a survey page that earned money for the scammer by the number of visits to that page.

Once you've clicked on a link, it's already too late. In some cases, software is already downloading something known as a Blackhole Exploit Kit. You'll never know it is downloading but the entire time it is scanning your computer looking for weaknesses. It can use your computer as a Botnet Zombie, it can steal information, or use key logging features to collect your passwords. It can do all sorts of things, depending on your computer's vulnerabilities.

I turned to LongURL Please (http://www.longurlplease.com) and installed it in my Firefox browser so that I can view the real destination of a shortened URL before I click on it. That helped reduce my sense of risk that I was going to click on a shortened URL that would take me to a scammer's malicious page. Another option is TheRealURL (http://therealurl.appspot.com/), which isn't rated as highly but you can pop a shortened URL right on their page to see the real URL link.

4. Twitter Work-At-Home Scam

Work-at-home scams have been around forever, well before the Internet, but they succeed at getting many more victims online than they did offline. Twitter is not protected from this scam. There are lots of identities on Twitter promoting their latest and greatest work-at-home scheme. And they may have a lot of followers – more than 100,000 for some of them, but this should not fool you. Followers do not necessarily translate into legitimacy. There are too many automated and fake accounts. It is easy to get a large number of "followers," who are probably not even live human beings. But scammers know a lot of people are fooled by the total number of followers. So they get a large number and then begin pitching their work-at-home "system."

Often in these schemes, first you are directed to their website where you have to give up information before you can read about the program (name, email address, zip code and sometimes even more). That's a red flag. If they can't talk about their program without collecting information on you, their program isn't worth reading about. Secondly, after you've given up your information, you will then be presented with the sales pitch, and for only $97 (as an example) you'll receive complete access to their "Wealth Development Center" (or whatever they are calling it). The goal is to get the $97 and then provide you access to crap, and make it really hard for you to get your $97 back.

Here are some work-at-home "tweets" that have been seen on Twitter (all with links to direct you to their scam website):

Check this out! I made -$19.97 today! - Home Wealth Formula Scam

Stay at home single mom makes $359/h. Work from home jobs. Check it out

Check out this article – I made $300 today!

CNN - Work at home mom makes $6,275/month working part-time from home

They will also send these messages via Direct Message. Report every one as spam.

Some of these scams have the goal to get you to respond to a simple offer – something free or for one penny. Or maybe an offer for a small shipping charge, but by agreeing to that, you have not taken the time to look at their small print and you've just agreed to a $49 a month automatic charge!

How do you protect yourself against these scams? Look at the fine print, don't pay for programs upfront unless you have thoroughly researched them, checked the Better Business Bureau (BBB.org), and search online to see what else has been said about their company name. Take your time and do your research. You don't have to agree to these things on a whim.

5. Twitter Phishing

Twitter is not immune from scammers using messages to trick you into giving up information you shouldn't be sharing, like passwords and your social security number. The ultimate goal of a phishing ("fishing") scammer is to get you to click on a link and begin filling out information, thinking you are on some website you trust when actually you are not. The most dangerous type of phishing involves getting you to click links that look like your online banking but are actually a bogus website with a confusing url. *customerservice-bankofamerica.com* is NOT the same thing as *bankofamerica.com*. Someone not paying attention might glance at that and think it is okay. Phishing scams happen with fake PayPal login pages, fake employment applications, fake entries to win a prize – scammers exploit every avenue they think you are likely to trust. On Twitter, messages with phishing links, as one approach, mimic the Twitter login page. By getting your Twitter login, they can then use your account to send out large Direct Messages, perhaps send more posts with links that could potentially infect other people's computers, or just get more information that would lead to bank accounts, PayPal account, etc. Always check where a link is going to take you before clicking on it.

6. Viruses and Spyware on Twitter

Viruses are software that actually do damage to the operation of your computer. Spyware is software that does not damage your computer, and mostly you won't even know it's there. But spyware monitors what you type and looks for account passwords that the scammer uses for draining your money accounts.

On Twitter, scammers will use messages, much like they do on Facebook, to try and trick you into clicking a link – and you want to, just to see why. For example, the message may say, *"OMG – did you see this photo you're in?"* and then provide a link that actually goes to a phishing page, or begins downloading malicious virus or spyware. If you got that message from a stranger you might think twice before clicking, but if the scammer has hacked into the account of someone you know, and then sent you that Direct Message, you are much more likely to click. Some of these phishing messages offer a way to know who has been looking at your Twitter profile but when you click on the link and download the "app," it doesn't tell you how many (or it just makes up a number), all the while installing spyware on your computer.

7. Other Twitter Scams

When on Twitter, be aware that all the scam variations I've discussed so far in this book so far can and probably will be present on Twitter in some form. I've seen the "Stranded Scam," where someone you know sends you a Direct Message saying they are stuck somewhere and need money wired to them. In fact, their account has been hacked by a scammer. I've seen the "Fake Seller Scam" on Twitter where you are talking about some product you are considering buying and suddenly you get a message from someone saying they have that item for sale at a great price. They don't, but they won't say that until they've gotten your credit card number to use in other illegal ways. I've seen the messages saying you've won a new iPhone and they just need your number so they can transfer your information. And what you've really just done is sign up for a monthly fee for some astrology service that will be almost impossible to stop. Lately, I've seen a lot of fake Twitter accounts that are used to spam users they are not even following by using people's Twitter handle and a link to an advertisement or phishing survey. For example, most of their Tweets will say something like, "@KTMObooks http://amzn.to/QsAzhT" (but in their case, they use many Twitter usernames with many Tweets and the links will all go to their advertisement or survey landing page). Scammers will set up hundreds of these fake accounts and Twitter can't take them down fast enough.

This book will help you become more capable of recognizing these scams before you do any clicking. My advice is to get a service that shows you the long real destination of a shortened URL on Twitter, and think, think, think, before clicking on any links. And I'll never be able to repeat this enough in this lifetime, do NOT wire anyone money. Period. Just don't do it.

CHAPTER 6: CRAIGLIST SCAMS

www.craigslist.com

I've ranked Craigslist number 5 for social media destination sites, with over 160 million estimated unique monthly visitors recorded in September 2012.. Craigslist actually began its history as a place to find out where the cool concerts and parties were in the San Francisco Bay Area. When they fleshed out more community sections, added classified advertisements, job listings, and expanded to more cities – the landscape of newspaper classifieds was changed forever (and doomed). Craigslist today remains a dominate force and a great place to sell your belongings, find cheap stuff, meet people, use their calendar of events, find housing, and scan for job openings. It is worldwide and well-known. It is commonly referenced in the news, although not always for good reasons – sometimes criminals actually get caught and say they used Craigslist to find their victims. Not always great press.

But still, Craigslist is a roaring success and all this success is going to eventually attract hordes of scammers. And attract them it did. You can reply to postings on the site while remaining relatively anonymous. Scammers can set up disposable email accounts and fake names and use those not only to post ads on Craigslist but also to pretend to be buyers and reply to hundreds and hundreds of seller postings, acting like they are going to buy whatever is being sold. Craigslist has become a lucrative playground for scammers. I sometimes wonder what percentages of all the replies to postings come from scammers. I don't know the number but I think if I did, it would be a scary big number.

Let's break down the major types of scams currently popular on Craigslist. I think you will see, after you read through this entire chapter, that you can use Craigslist safely and confidently. You just need to look for a handful of Red Flag Clues so that you know you are dealing with a legitimate person and not a scammer.

1. Fake Buyer Scam

Because Craigslist is a successful place to post ads to sell your stuff, probably the most common scam running is the fake buyer scam. Actually, the fake buyer scam can be found on any commerce site, but I'll cover this scam here as it is found on Craigslist.

In the fake buyer scam, the scammer will respond to as many ads as their little fingers can handle. Scammers have templates they use so the emails will look very similar, except for minor variations. They will plug in the name of the item in their template and create what looks to be a customized personal email but it will contain some obvious red flags. If you become familiar with these red flags, it should be relatively easy for you recognize these emails and separate them from legitimate customer responses.

How It Works:

The scammer will typically send a "feeler" email to the seller first. This email will say something like, *"Is this item still available?"* You could have several items listed for sale on Craigslist and you will still likely receive some email that says, *"Im interested in the posted item, I hope it is in good condition?"* (apostrophe missing on purpose because scammers are notorious for their bad grammar and spelling), *"Are you the direct seller?"* They are waiting to narrow their focus to those people who reply. And once the seller does reply, the scammer now has the seller's email address. He can always add that to his database and sell these addresses to other scammers. The item you are selling really doesn't matter. And neither does the price, though scammers love to go after the high-ticket items because then they can scam their victims for that much more money. But they will really go after any seller on Craigslist because the scam is not about the item.

So far, my experience has shown that legitimate potential buyers always include their name and often their phone number within their first initial email. And when I google their email address, I can usually find some reference to it online. Not always, but usually. The key here is that, in general, legitimate buyers typically provide a bit more information in their initial email, often use a longer sentence when asking a question, and many include their phone number so it can be verified.

The second email response from a scammer is also a template and only sent to those sellers who have replied to the first email. The scammer will now have a bit of a problem. Craigslist puts the full title of the item in the subject line so they scammer knows exactly what item this potential victim is selling. Now they can personalize their emails more. I often remove all references to the item when replying to a scammer but have learned this doesn't bother them at all, they will go ahead and send their templated second response. The second response will mention the next stage of the scam – they will ask you to remove the listing, and they will want to pay with a certified check and they need your address to send their check.

A typical second response from a scammer might look like this:

EXAMPLE EMAIL:

Hi,

I really appreciate your response .I want you to consider it sold,Please do withdraw the advert from CL to avoid disturbance,anyway I don't have time to come over to take a look because of my Business but you don't need to bother yourself with the shipment, I'll take care of that by engaging the services of my mover, hence I'll be sending a check and it will be delivered to you via United Parcel Service, so I'll need you to provide me with the following information to facilitate the mailing of the check.

1.full name on the check.

2.Full Physical address to post the check

3.City, State and Zip Code

4.Home & Cell Phone to contact you.

Note that the payment will be shipped to your address and once again I will like you to know that you will not be responsible for shipping i have my mover that will expedite the pick up as soon as you have cashed the check,N.B UPS does not deliver to a P.O box addresses.

Regards

Michael

What they are doing in this second email is setting up the absolutely critical part of this scam – overpaying on the amount owed and asking the seller to forward the difference to pay a non-existent shipper, always via a wire transfer. Their payment will turn out to be a counterfeit money order or check, or a stolen credit card number (not yet reported as stolen), or a falsified email saying PayPal has received their payment when the scammer never paid PayPal at all.

This is where most sellers get suspicious and I have to say, some become actual victims because they over-ride their gut instinct, which is telling them something is not right. Those who talk themselves out of what their gut is telling them usually do this because:

- they are a giving/generous type of person and feel compelled to help a buyer out so the sale works out

- they are desperate for money or desperate to offload an item and so they "push" forward with the sale

- they generally believe people do not lie about their story or intentions, so they are somewhat naïve

If the seller actually replies to this second email, the third step of the scam is for the scammer to send payment. Again, this will happen one of three ways: (1) check or money, (2) credit card, or (3) PayPal. None of these payment methods will be legitimate. The check will be counterfeit, or the credit card will be stolen (and often not yet reported so it will actually clear but will always result in a chargeback). Or they will fake a PayPal confirmation email hoping you won't take the time to actually check your PayPal to see if the payment is actually there. Scammers will have mentioned about their shipping company but won't say anything else about that until the seller suddenly receives a check for way more than what is owed, typically by a difference of $1000-$5000. The buyer will provide instructions on how to forward the money to their shipping company (remember, there is no shipping company) and it will *always* involve a wire transfer (like Western Union or MoneyGram). Why? Because once the scammer picks up your forwarded money, they and the money are completely untraceable and your money is gone.

Here is a full exchange from a seller on Craigslist and "Bruce" who is a scam buyer. Notice how in the eighth email, the scammer escalated to outright threats. A scammer is never going to report you to any authorities. They are hoping against hope that perhaps you have a fear of authority and out of fear you will go ahead and wire them the money.

EXAMPLE EMAIL:

First email from Bruce: Still Available???

Second email from Bruce: Am glad it's available. I'm going on a vacation but I will instruct my assistant to prepare and mail your payment which I'm sure you will get in about 4 - 5 business days. I'll add $50 extra for the delay. I'll pay by M O or cashier check so send me your info (i.e full name, mailing address and your phone number) so payment can be mailed out immediately. I will also make arrangement for pick-up which will be after you must have received and cashed the payment.Please take the posting off craigs list today and consider it sold to me.Expecting to hear from you soon.

Thanks

Third email from Bruce: Hi, Thanks for your quick mail,Your payment has been sent but there is something i think i must bring to your notice immediately. I just discovered there is an error in the payment sent to you. My Assistant sent the payment meant for another item thats more expensive than yours. I have called the post office to see if they could retrieve it but nothing positive. I really dont know what to do now. Please and Please, you can go ahead and cash out the Money Order at your Bank when you receive it, deduct your payment and send the balance via western union to the details i will provide you with. Can i trust you to do that for me?

Thanks

Fourth email from Bruce: The pickup we be after my parent cleared your bank okay?

Fifth email from Bruce: Hi, Thanks for putting my mind at rest. I am sure you will get payment (3-4 working days). So please let me know when you receive it so i can tell you where to send my balance and also schedule date for pick-up. Looking forward to completing this transaction with you as soon as possible.please NOTE:western union charges should be deducted from my remaining balance after deducting your fee for the item.western union my balance to the details i will provide you with

Thanks

Sixth email from Bruce: Please let me know if you have received payment I am in London at the moment. If you have, you can go ahead and get it cashed at your bank, deduct your payment and send the balance via western union to the following details:

NAME OF RECEIVER: BRUCE MILLER

ADDRESS:5 Westminster Bridge Road

CITY: LONDON

COUNTRY: UNITED KINGDOM

ZIP CODE: SE1 7XW

Please make sure you take care of everything sameday and send me the transfer details i.e Money Transfer Control Number (MTCN) and the total amount sent after charges. I will need the money to take care of some pressing bills and pay for pick-up.

Seventh email from Bruce: Deduct whatever the charges is from my left amount

Eighth email from Bruce: PLEASE LET ME KNOW WHAT IS GOING ON. I NEED TO HEAR FROM YOU ASAP

BECAUSE I WILL BE REPORTING THIS TO THE APPROPRIATE AUTHORITIES IN THE NEXT 24HOURS IF I DONT HEAR FROM YOU.I NEED MY WESTERN UNION TRANSFER DETAILS IIF YOU HAVE SENT MY BALANCE OVER.

Here are some more actual responses from fake buyers:

Hi,

Am glad it's available. I'm going on a business trip to London but I will instruct my assistant to prepare and mail your payment which I'm sure you will get in about 5 - 7 business days. I'll add $30 extra for the delay. I can only pay via money order as am going on a business trip now so send me your info (i.e full name, mailing address and your phone number) so payment can be mailed out immediately. I will also make arrangement for pick-up which will be after you must have received and cashed the payment. Awaiting your info.

Thanks

and

Hello,My assistant told me your item is still for sale on list, I will add $50 to the purchase price for you so that you can hold it for me as i am on a business trip and wouldn't want to lose it to someone else. Please provide your full name, address and your phone number so that I can send your payment.I will be paying you by a Money Order ... It will take 6 -7 days for the payment to get to you and as for delivery I will make arrangements for the pick-up after you have received payment.kindly get back to me, as soon as possible, with your name,phone # and mailing

```
address where payment will be sent.Note:As
soon as you have your money in hand, we can
talk about the picking up of the item. i would
like you to take the posting off from
craiglist today.
```

Are you beginning to see the red flag clues?

Scam Alert Red Flag Clues

- Once the buyer starts explaining they have their own shipper who will be handling their "move," they are likely a scammer.

- If the buyer has a story that includes overpaying and you forwarding money to someone else or back to them, do not proceed.

- If any part of the transaction involves using wire transfer services like Western Union or MoneyGram, do not proceed.

- For high-priced items, if the buyer is not local and/or has some story why they can not come see the item in person, do not proceed. Often they will say they are out of the country or buying it for a relative as a way of getting out of you verifying their identity.

Once a seller gets a check for more than the amount, many sellers will finally listen to their instinct and try googling to see if they can verify anything about the person or their story. But some sellers will continue along the scam path and land in stage 4 of the scam, which is they deposit the check or process the credit card and then take their own good money and forward it via Western Union according to the instructions of the buyer. At this point, the scam is pretty much complete and the scammer and the seller's money disappear and scammers move on to their other potential victims.

Some variations you will find on this are:

- the buyer will pay for an item with a counterfeit check or stolen credit card and just disappear after getting the item shipped to them. This is not the usual motivation for a scammer, who is typically less interested in the item than the cash they can get from the scam, but some scammers are just into buying things with counterfeit checks and bad credit cards.

- the buyer will pay for an item with a counterfeit check, pay more than the amount owed and act like they got confused about the amount, or the wife or secretary wrote it out for the wrong amount, and then they ask you to wire the difference back to them. Their money is bad; your money that you forward is good, and gone.

How To Avoid This Scam:

- Do not accept overpayments

- Do not forward money in anyone's behalf

- Do not use wire transfer services for your deals

- If they pay by PayPal, always manually check your PayPal account before shipping the product – don't just take their word that they paid or believe some "email confirmation," log in yourself and check

- For high-priced items, only deal locally and insist the person come see the item first

- Responses with a local phone number that can be verified are more likely to be real – be sure and check the phone number

2. Fake Seller Scam

Not only is Craigslist an attractive platform for scam buyers, it is also a place scammers will pretend to be sellers. They have nothing to sell but they pretend they do, in order to scam money out of unsuspecting buyers. I'll cover a couple of distinct Fake Seller Scams prevalent when using Craigslist and hopefully, as a buyer, I can keep you from falling victim to them.

Fake Car Seller

Craigslist can be a source of great car deals and a lot of people turn to Craigslist when they are looking for used cars. Scammers know this and so scammers will post ads selling cars that do not exist, taking photos from other sources online. They put an excellent price on the cars and hope to attract interested buyers to reply to the ad. Once a potential victim replies to the advertisement, the scammer will attempt to get that buyer to send a deposit on the car – either directly to them, or if they sense the victim is hesitating, they will set up a fake escrow with a name that sounds like a real one and get the buyer to wire the deposit to the fake escrow account.

In a similar approach, a scam seller will have a long backstory about how and why they are selling a car and that they are currently not in the country (or they are selling in behalf of an ill relative and doing it from another country, going through a divorce and currently out of the country) and then ask the buyer to wire the money to them to take possession of the car and, of course, once the money is wired the buyer finds out there is no car and their money is gone.

Fake House Seller

It is common for scammers to just grab photos online of houses that are on the market and put an ad up on Craigslist and act like they are selling that house, and they will put a really attractive price on it. In actuality, they have no legitimate right to be representing selling that house, but that is not the point of the scam. The point is to get a "deposit" out of you to hold the house and not sell it someone else. And once you send the deposit (they will always have some story around why it needs to be sent via wire transfer, such as Western Union or MoneyGram), it is gone and the scammer will disappear.

Some scammers try and use an escrow service to trick their victims into believing the deal is now more "secure." But it is not. The scammer will instruct the buyer to send the money to the escrow account and they proceed to send the victim a fake email that looks like the real thing from a real escrow company (escrow.com, for example) but it is not. The email will have a link which goes to a bogus website where the victim – thinking they are at the website of a legitimate escrow service, will fill out information and send money to a fake escrow account and the victim's money is gone.

Fake Rental Ads

This section of Craigslist is pretty lucrative for scammers. It needs its own section in my book because so many people are falling for this scam. Watch for the recurring themes of how the criminals approach these scams.

A scammer will steal some lovely photo of a home or apartment for rent. Often they will steal the description from some pre-existing ad. There will be a price that is too good to believe but not so great that it is completely unbelievable. The problem is the scammer has no association with the listed place and is just using it to scam money out of unsuspecting victims. With such a great price on a place that looks great in the photos, a number of people will reply to the advertisement. Then the "landlord" (who is just the scammer) will explain there are a number of people ready to snatch it up but if they will wire the deposit with first and last month's rent, the place is theirs (the scammer says that to everyone who replies, increasing his take). Once the money is wired, the scammer disappears and so does the money.

> A man in Santa Maria, CA saw an ad on Craiglist for $1000. He thought that was an amazing price and he

> immediately replied, thinking it would get snapped up quickly. He checked out the address. The scammer replied and said that because they were currently out of the country, they wanted to know more about their potential renter and asked for a lot of personal information - his job, his income, his family. Then the scammer asked for the first month's rent and the deposit, $2000, to be wired to them. The potential renter complied. The rental agreement never came but another request for $1000 for last month's rent did come, asking it be wired again. Finally, the potential renter got suspicious. He went online and found out the property had just sold and had never been available for rent.

This is one example how dealing with an unseen entity who is out of the country is very likely a scam.

A variation of this scam is a "landlord" showing a foreclosure place for rent. The landlord is really a scammer who has broken into a foreclosed house owned by a bank and pretending he owns it. So in this case, a scammer is even able to show the place face-to-face and will have some story as to why he needs the money in cash or wired. In many cases, tenants have actually moved into these places and lived there a month or two until the bank figures it out and informs them the bank owns the house or condo and there was no agent or landlord renting it out. This version is particularly despicable.

There is also the version of the "middleman," a scammer pretending to be the agent for the owner who is out of country, or perhaps on an extended stay in the hospital or recovery, or acting in behalf of a relative who lives some place far away. None of these things will be true, but once the potential renter has given them money, the scammer will disappear and the renter will find out the place was never actually for rent.

Also, keep in mind that these rental scams do not always come from fake landlords and agents. Sometimes, scammers act like potential renters and try to steal money from unsuspecting landlords. In these cases, the scammer will use the typical strategy of trying to overpay for the deposit and first and last month's rent with a counterfeit check, claim they miswrote the check (or their wife or secretary did), and ask the landlord to wire back the difference to them. If the landlord moves too quickly through this process and agrees to send back the difference, via wire transfer, it will be too late when they discover the original funds were counterfeit.

Here is an actual example of a first email received by a landlord who had placed a rental ad on Craigslist:

EXAMPLE EMAIL:

```
My name is lovety and I am looking to rent a
place to live. I am a young professional and
will be needing to move ASAP. I am willing to
pay first and last months rent .I am very
responsible and open to any kind of lease. I
am an Humanitarian worker and was posted on a
new job to your area.I will be glad if i could
hear back from you sooner.

Thank You
```

How To Avoid The Housing Rental Scam:

- Do a quick search of the person's name and email address who is handling the transaction with you. If they have scammed others under the same name, you might quickly find validation of that online and instantly decide to stop right there.

- You want to make sure the landlord is the legitimate owner of the house, condo or apartment. If it is a house, you can easily do a property search on Google and see who is the current owner. If the name doesn't match, do not proceed. If they say they are an agent, get the contact name of the owner and contact them to verify it is really available. If it is a condo, there is typically a homeowners association or property management company – contact them and verify the condo is really available for rent. And if it is an apartment, verify ownership or if a management company is handling the property, look up the company independently and call them to verify the information you were given.

- The scammer landlord will likely not even ask you to fill out an application or run a credit check. They will focus more on you paying the deposit in order to secure a place in high demand. Some may go through the motions of mentioning the application or credit check but never get around to doing that with you. If it seems too easy and no background check is done, do some more research on your landlord before proceeding.

- If you are a landlord, do not ever accept checks that are over the amount owed. And never agree to forward back money to anyone via wire transfer. And never return any money until a bank has agreed the check is not fraudulent (which is different than the bank accepting it for deposit – some counterfeit checks take weeks to be found out and you are still responsible for the amount).

- If you are a landlord, before offering a lease, be sure and do a full background check, credit checks, criminal histories, etc.

- Even if the potential renter is local and wants to come see an apartment, never see a prospective tenant alone. Always have someone with you. Same goes for the prospective tenants as well – do not go alone.

Fake Ticket Sales

Craigslist is a great source for secondary market tickets for concerts and sporting events and even travel tickets, but this is one of the scammers' favorite ways to steal money from victims. There are two main approaches to stealing money via fake tickets, but you can be sure more variations of these will evolve.

Counterfeit Tickets – in this approach, scammers use their computer and printers and create realistic-looking tickets and sell them to unsuspecting buyers. Sometimes it is only when the buyer shows up at an event that he or she finds out their seat either doesn't exist or was sold to another person with a real ticket. When scammers go for big money, they will counterfeit tickets which are in high demand (and thus can charge a lot) or season tickets which cost sometimes thousands of dollars.

A flag of any of these scams is that the scammer will have some story as to why they need the money wired to them, thus making the money untraceable once it has been picked up. Also, don't fall for any email that says Craigslist has reviewed this seller and approved them. Craigslist doesn't provide any evaluation of sellers or buyers.

Cancelled Tickets – this scam may use concert or sporting events, but also targets airline tickets. Here is how it works: the scammer will use a stolen credit card to purchase a ticket, and this card will often not yet be reported as stolen yet so actually "works." They then immediately post an ad on Craigslist and get a buyer to buy that ticket. They'll have some made-up story as to why they are not using that ticket themselves. As soon as the buyer pays them, they go back and cancel the ticket but the buyer doesn't know that until they show up at the airport or concert event and find that the ticket was cancelled. And because it was the scammer who sold them the ticket, the buyer has no recourse. When the security at airports changed, it no longer is possible to "transfer" tickets from one person to another, so scammers just altered this scam to sell airline ticket "vouchers." Also be careful of references to "US Airlines" tickets. There is no such airline.

How To Avoid The Ticket Sales Scam:

It is important to know what the ticket is supposed to look like in order to know if what you have been sent is a counterfeit ticket. Ask the seller to send a photo of the ticket before you purchase it. It is easy enough to do these days with a smartphone or digital camera.

For the ticket image the seller has sent you, look online for the seating plan and match the row and numbers to what has been put on your ticket and see if it matches or makes sense.

Verify the ticket has been purchased. Ask the seller to send a copy or image of the invoice or receipt for the purchased ticket(s). If they can't or don't want to, it's best not to proceed. Sometimes scammers will take the time to forge a receipt and send that to you. Call the event's host and verify it is a valid ticket. This is particularly important if you are buying season tickets for the symphony or baseball. Sometimes the scammer will have a receipt, but it is only for one ticket and they are attempting to sell you season tickets from that receipt for one ticket.

Tickets via Mail – when receiving tickets via mail, do not pay the full amount upfront, unless you've done your homework and feel comfortable the tickets are for real. You can try and offer to pay for half upfront and half upon receipt. Of course the seller may move on to someone who doesn't have that request but better to be safe with no tickets than scammed with faked tickets. Ask that the tickets be sent with a tracking number.

3. Employment Scams

Given the really tough economic conditions and how many people are out of work or underemployed, scammers are exploiting a weak spot in a really terrible way – stealing money from those looking for work. People looking for a job are particularly vulnerable to scammers because they are likely to be more desperate and in more need of money. They may be more likely to over-ride their gut instinct, which is telling them something is not right. Scammers know this. While many scam job openings are typically work-at-home opportunities, this scam has become so pervasive, it can be found as postings that look like perfectly legitimate corporate jobs. Seniors and people who have been retired are particularly susceptible, as they are looking for ways to supplement their fixed income and are not typically familiar with how a scammer might exploit their trust and emotions.

Let's take a look at the common scams being perpetrated on Craigslist in the jobs section so that you can recognize them and not become a victim.

1. **Payroll Assistant Scam**

This is probably one of the most common employment scams on Craigslist, because it directly works what is known as the "check cashing" scam. The scammer ends up hiring people to do their money laundering for them and the person never knows it. Often they suspect something is fishy about what they are doing but they think it's a job and they are thankful for having a job, so they do it.

How It Works:

The scammer will post an ad on Craigslist that appears to be a real job opportunity. One of the common titles often used is "Payroll Assistant". The scammer's first email will describe the job and pay, much like a real advertisement, and wait for people to reply to their ad. When someone does, the scammer's second email will have some story as to why you will be communicating with them on their personal email. They move forward with trying to collect as much of your private financial and banking information as they can, under the guise of their application process.

If you fall all the way through this scam, they will then begin either sending you counterfeit checks to be resent elsewhere or they will have you print out counterfeit checks right on your printer and mail them to the destination they specify. At this point, you are basically helping them with their scams when they mail counterfeit checks to victims (making the postmark a more local address), as well as move counterfeit checks around to other scammers.

A day or two before you are expecting to be paid, the scammer will disappear and set up another victim to do this work for them. Sometimes, before disappearing, the scammer will try and get you to cash one of the checks and wire the difference back to them – and that check will also be counterfeit. This will be the final insult as they steal money from you instead of paying you for your work, and then disappear.

Here is an example of the email reply when someone replied to an ad on Craigslist for a Payroll Assistant:

EXAMPLE EMAIL:

Am Mrs Merrell, My professional job is payroll ,I have been into this business for few years back,Now i think i need assistant who will be helping me with this payroll stuff,this job take most of my time and i think i need to spend most of my time with my children this time around,that is why am in need to helper.

Have you ever been into payroll work before,well i dont think that should be the problem as am sure this work is very easy to lean LOL.

-WAGES AND BENEFITS-

I will be paying you $1300 monthly salary by working from your home,A little about the job.

I use to get contract from company and they ask me to send payroll check to their (Customer)(Client)(Workers), So you will be responsible for that, you will be mailling the check out to those client via UPS.com, You will be doing this job in your home,I think this job is a great opportunity for you,and it doesnt requir any specific time,you can work any time you like in a day, you can also do this at night and send them out next morning if you are busy during the day, Note that we will be responsible for the postage.

Before you start this job, you will need to get below materials,youb are going to use the materials to start your job.

Colored Printer

```
Scanner

Versa Gold 2010 software

Versa Paper Check

Brown letter size envelope

Magnetic or regular Ink

Your personal computer

Note that every material you buy would be
reimbursed along with your first salary.

Please if you are interested and want to know
more about this job, please kindly chat with
me on my yahoo IM via(jodiemerrell@yahoo.com)
i stay online from 7am to 11am everyday.if you
dont have a yahoo IM please kindly set up one
so you be able to chat with me.

Response from you would highly appreciated.

Thanks for your interest.
```

And following is an email exchange where the initial job listing was for a Computer Technician, but when the job seeker got a reply back, the email began referring to a Payroll Assistant. This was a certain tip-off that something was not right with this job opportunity.

EXAMPLE EMAIL:

```
Computer Technician

We are looking for a responsible adult who is
in search of a rewarding long-term commitment
in the IT field. This is a PC Tech. position.
The job candidate must be a self-motivated
quick learner with a strong PC skill set.
```

```
Great on the job training available.

Job responsibilities;

PC Installation/Configuration/Troubleshooting

Basic Server/Networking
Installation/Configuration/Troubleshooting

Run, route in & terminate Voice/Video/Data
cabling

Advancement Opportunity;

The chosen job applicant will have an
opportunity to learn many new technologies by
working with multiple clients with diverse
needs.

Principals only. Recruiters, please don't
contact this job poster.

Please, no phone calls about this job!

Please do not contact job poster about other
services, products or

commercial interests.

PostingID: 2265034183
```

and here is their reply, which threw red flags up when the scammer began discussing a Payroll Assistant job. One can clearly see their poor sentence structure and how they set up the scenario that you will be receiving checks from them and sending those checks elsewhere (the checks are counterfeit):

EXAMPLE EMAIL:

Hello,

I am Charles Stenger, CPA, MBA. I run a private accounting firm and am currently looking to strengthen my organizational structure by adding a Personal Assistant that would work part time as a Payroll assistant i am presently sick, i have stroke and hypertension, so i require a person who will be honest, trustworthy and able to work hard who will handle the printing of Payroll-Checks with the data information of our client on payroll list of the company co-workers and which will be done under the authorization of the company which is legalized by Government in which we will be made for you to dispatch the checks to our client various destinations in USA and i will take care of the shipping and handling of the payrolls you are dropping off.

Secondly, you are only to do these two processes, printing and dispatching, so i will like to know if you will be trustworthy enough to entrust mine and my clients company's vital information and signatory with you, please we want you to be sure that we will be paying you $350 weekly salary for a start (you will only be working 4 to 5 hours per each day, if you performed very well, we will increase your salary to $650 as your performances impress me after a couple of months so, please get back to me today to know your interest.

DO CONFIRM ACCEPTANCE OF THIS POSITION BY PROVIDING BELOW DETAILS. DECLINE THE OFFER BY NOT REPLYING, OR SAYING NO.

PLEASE FILL THE APPLICATION FORM BELOW:

First Name :__________________

Middle Name:__________________

Last Name:__________________

Full Street Address(not PO BOX)
:__________________

City:__________________

State:__________________

Zip Code:__________________

Cell Phone Number:__________________

Home Phone Number:__________________

Email Address:__________________

Present Work/Position:__________________

What date are you available to start work?
(Immediately)

Regards,

Charles

A scam is obvious when the scammer can't keep their scam emails straight, changing their job titles mid-stream, but other times it is not so easy to see a scam. Look for the angle of their story about processing checks and sending them elsewhere. This type of job, when done from home, is almost always a scam job doing money laundering. And you'd be committing the felony of mail fraud if you mail any checks via USPS.

2. **Shipping Assistant Scam**

When scammers use stolen credit cards to buy things, they need to have a local country address to have them shipped to, and then they need some way to get those same items shipped out of the country to them. It is typically things like electronics but can be any high-ticket items, like jewelry or sporting equipment.

So, in this version of a job scam, the scammer hires people to receive items in their behalf and ship those items elsewhere for them, typically to foreign countries. That is why this scam is referred to as the "Re-Ship Scam." The job title they will advertise for is something like "Shipping Assistant," "Merchandising Manager," or "Package Processing Assistant." If someone falls for this scam, they become complicit in the crime of moving stolen goods; people in the U.S. have been arrested for this because it is a felony. Victims sometimes say they thought something was weird about the job but they needed the extra money, or sometimes they did it knowing full well what they were doing since the scammer let them keep some of the stolen goods, like TV's, etc. When the credit card is finally reported as stolen, the authorities will first pursue who they can – and that is usually person who has been receiving and shipping the stolen goods. The scammer typically disappears without a trace.

EXAMPLE EMAIL:

Hi!

My name is Dennis and i represent Mail&Fulfillment LLC. We are a logistics company which provides services for goods receiving and handling and also mail forwarding. Your candidacy was provided by online recruiter for position of Commodity Inspector.

Position requirements:

- Be USA citizen

- Flexible schedule

- Legal age

- Skills or experience with PC

- Responsibility

We offer competitive salary, excellent benefits, and flexible schedule. We do not require a special education to start working, but we expect our candidates be extremely motivated, be attentive to detail, a positive attitude.

For more information about the post please write to our manager by email: dennis.grossman@mnfllcmail.com with your contact details and convenient way to communicate.

Best Regards,

Dennis Grossman,

Mail & Fulfillment LLC

The job seeker in this case was not sure why he received this email but he was looking for a job, so he replied and attached his resume and cover letter. This is the email he got back:

Hello!

My name is Dennis Grossman. I am a hiring manager of Mail & Fulfillment LLC. You responded to our request on the open position. At this moment our company is looking for a Commodity Inspector and we will be glad to consider you for this position. Let me provide you more information about the position we offer. All the details are put together into one file, which you can find attached to this email. To decide if you like this position or if you suit our requirements, please, begin with reading the job specs in the attached file. I want to add some important points. First of all, I must say, that you will work in your city and you don't need to visit the office of the company. All the tasks you will receive in the Internet or by phone. Secondly, I must emphasize, that we appreciate loyalty and diligence. If you work conscious and complete the tasks in time, you will get bonuses to the base salary and you will also get career opportunities. I hope, this information will help you to make a choice.

If you decided to accept this offer, you need to go through a hiring process:

Step 1. Fill in the application form and send it to me via e-mail. Mind that we do not accept CV or any other documents. You will be considered only within this application form. Because of being recommended by an on-line recruiting agency, you will get on a priority basis.

Step 2. We will make a decision over your employment and send you a notice. If decision is positive, we will send you an official confirmation that you are hired for this position, Employment Agreement, which you will have to sign. If you have some questions, we will give you a call to discuss the details.

Step 3. When signed the agreement, you become an official employee of our company and can get to work. You will have a Supervisor, who will put you into the workflow.

So, if you are ready to start the hiring process, please, read the job specs, then fill in the application form and send it to me.

I also advise you to add my email address to the contact list to be sure, that my letters reach you.

Dennis.

3. Fake Employment Agencies

There are plenty of employment agencies out there which provide valuable services to job seekers. An employment agency can have relationships with companies you may want to work for and they also provide a source of on-going intel of the opportunities that are in the marketplace.

But in spite of all the good employment agencies, there are also those disreputable firms that are more focused on selling their services than they are in placing candidates in jobs.

There are two main ways fake or unscrupulous agencies take your money. One way is to promise to send your resume to their special list of company contacts, for a fee. They really don't have any special list and they also attempt to collect as much personal information on you as they can. The other way is to charge fees for "testing" your skill sets and that is their revenue stream, not placing you in a job.

In separating the good agencies from those agencies you want to avoid, here are some things to look for:

- When you've been given the company name of an agency, take the time to look them up and see if you can verify more information about them. Check WHOIS and see who their website domain is registered to. Check the BBB. Check references to it online. Scammers tend to hide information about their bogus website and name while real agencies do not.

- If you have recently posted your resume online and suddenly an employment agency has found you and has the perfect job for you, do your research on the agency first. Often this can just be an agency trying to sell their fee-based add-on services (like testing) rather than placing you in a job.

- Do not believe you have been offered a job unless you have received written proof of the offer and get the phone number of your future employer (or if you know the name, just call the

HR department). Call and confirm the position is open and you are being offered the position.

- Legitimate employment agencies make money when a candidate has been placed in a job or a percentage of the hourly wage for contractors. They do not make money by charging upfront fees for services. Do not pay for testing services. Even if you require a test for a certification, do this outside the agency on your own. Do not pay to have your resume redone by that agency. If you want help with your resume, you can pay someone who offers those services independently of the agency. Do not pay for any special seminar that the agency says is "required."

4. **Fake Job Applications and Offers**

In this scam, the job listing may look perfectly legitimate and even the company name is that of a real company. Often the job will be something like Marketing Manager or Accounting Assistant. The details of the job are listed and everything looks normal. What the scammer has done is just stolen the text of someone else's job ad and posted it as their own. When you reply, they will send an email back saying something like, "Great, we'd like to proceed but because our clients are so sensitive, we'll need to do a background check first." They then either attach an official-looking form or just put the information they need right in the body of the email. The tip off is they ask for personal information that a legitimate employer would never ask for in email, like your social security number, your credit card numbers, your bank account numbers. What the scammer is after is stealing your identity and raiding your bank account. They will ask for every piece of information they would need to falsely their identity using your information.

You can usually tell if a job posting is a scam by the first reply you get. Real employers do not hire without meeting you, asking for a resume, and doing an interview. Real employers do not ask, and in some of those items, *legally* can not ask such personal financial information. And again, if you can't meet the person at the company location in a face-to-face meeting, run away from that job opportunity.

In the following actual email example, there are a couple of flags. Notice how the scammer immediately tries to explain away why you are replying to a personal email (which is just a disposable account the scammer set up for this scam), instead of to company email. Notice how the scammer tries to move the victim through the scam quickly. Notice how the scammer has a fax number set up to receive the forms with all the victim's personal information on it (always check the destination of a fax number before faxing anyone personal information – but my better advice would be never to fax anyone your personal financial information). And notice how, at the end, the scammer attempts to get the victim's bank PIN number. Oh, it's a risk, but when most people are asked to give a 4 digit code, they'll give up the same four digits as they use at their bank. All the scammer needs is one or two people who actually do this. What is the "payment code" referred to in the following email? It might be a way the scammer is tracking what they said to whom, because they send out hundreds of thousands of these emails. Scammers also mention setting up an in-person interview – and that will make it seem very legitimate, but the scam will be completed well before then and the scammer will have all the victim's information in hand and, at that point, just disappear.

EXAMPLE EMAIL:

```
Thank you for applying for the Marketing
Manager position with CIGNA Health Insurance.
I just had a chance to review your resume and
am going to send your application through for
hiring. If you are not interested in the job
please let me know no later than Wednesday so
I can look at other candidates.The position
will start in 3 weeks, and pay is negotiable
so you will need to start thinking about your
salary requirements so we can discuss them
later this week. I would like to give you a
call, what's the best time to reach you and at
what number? You can email me at my personal
account, which is cignahrdir@safe-mail.net. My
office line is 1-310-323-5481.The position
will require a background check because of the
nature of the high level of security that we
have with our clients. I am attaching the form
in this email. Just open it up, fill it out,
```

and fax it back to 1-775-623-7128, that's a secured fax line to the company that handles all the screening. They usually take a few days to get them done, so if you could get it done by Wednesday I would appreciate it. Email me when you're through, and we can go from there.The payment code, which goes on, the application is: 2644-2052-4689-4919. If you don't put that on there they wont process it, or maybe they will get in touch with you and try to get you to pay for the screening, so make sure you don't forget to put the payment info on there so they can bill us for it.I will need to also set up an in person interview with you, and would like to get it done by Friday. Are there any days that don't/won't work for you? If there are any problems email them to me, and either me or my assistant, Christy Anderson will get back with you.I look forward to meeting you and I will talk to you early next week.

Sincerely,

Russell C. Smith

Human Resources Director

CIGNA Health Insurance

PS. I am going to set up an account for you on our secure server so you can access our site and projects. Email me a four digit (have to be numbers no letters) so I can set it as your pass code. Your username will be your first middle and last name. You can change it once I set the account up. Email that to me as well if you would. Thanks again and have a great week.

5. **Mystery Shopper Scam**

The mystery shopper scam packages a check-cashing scam as if it is a job opportunity in order to lure in victims. If you reply to an ad on Craigslist for a mystery shopper, the scammer will send an email that looks official and explains they are looking for mystery shoppers in your area. If you check out the website, often they have also set up a bogus website to make it all look official. If you reply that you are interested and provide your mailing address, they will send the first check, typically in some amount like $3750, as an example (it will usually be some large but odd amount to make it seem more legitimate). Their company name will be fake but will sound official, something like "Experian Research Associates." They will instruct you to deposit this check, take $200 for yourself (or they will say $200 goes to them as a training fee), use $300 as a mystery shopper, and wire the remainder back to them (or their story will say you are forwarding the money to their local headquarters). They sometimes will say (or even send you) a form to fill out about your shopping experience.

You may have already wired the difference back to the scammer, and you may have even spent $300 of your own money buying things as a mystery shopper. But what you will then find out is that the original check sent to you was counterfeit, and you are now on the hook for the entire $3750 of your own money and the scammer has disappeared.

Here is an actual example of this type of scam:

EXAMPLE EMAIL:

Hello,

My Name is Mrs Kelly Clark.You have been selected for assignment as a Detective Shopper in your area and I am glad to inform and congratulate you as a member of our working team.

Once again we will like you to Re-confirm your details:

1. Full Name :

2. Addresss :

3. City:

4.State,

5. Country, :

& ZIP

6.Occupation :

7.Age :

8. E-Mail :

9. Cell and Home Phone :

Secret Shopper duty is fun and rewarding, and There is no charge to become a shopper and you do not need previous experience.

We serve clients across the United States Of America with over 500,000 shoppers available and ready to help businesses better serve their customers.

Stores and organizations such as The Gap, Walmart, Pizza Hut,Western Union and Bank. One amongst many others pay for Secret Shopper to shop in their establishments and report their experiences. We NEVER charge fees to be a shopper.

JOB DESCRIPTION

ASSIGNMENT PACKET :

Before any assignment we would provide you with the resources needed {cash}Mostly,you would be sent a check,which you can cash and use for the assignment. Included to the check would be your assignment packet Then we would be providing you details on here. But you follow every single information given to you as a secret shopper .

PAYMENT TERMS:

Your payment would be sent to you per Assignment which is ($250) Also you will be provided with all expense money for the shopping and other expenses incurred during the course of your assignment.All the tools you will needing would be provided to you with details on every assignment.

There have been reports about lapses in these companies or stores services of their management and some of their staffs. The complaints are based on reports which the customers forward anonymously.

For the following reasons:

I) Rudeness to customers

ii) Slow services

iii) Poor services

THANK YOU FOR YOUR TIME AND EFFICIENCY.YOUR RESPONSE IS NEEDED TO FACILITATE THAT YOU UNDERSTAND THE INSTRUCTION.

We look forward to working with you and await your prompt response

Regards

Mrs Kelly Clark

Sometimes the scammer doesn't mess around and gets you to "assess" Western Union by depositing their check and then wiring the rest of the money to see how Western Union performs. This approach is for lazy scammers because they don't have to work hard for their stolen money in this case. Here is someone who replied to a mystery shopper ad on Craigslist but caught on just in the nick of time:

I was looking for a job on Craigslist and answered an ad for a mystery shopper. I thought it was legit because I have known people that have done this. I received an email back saying that I was hired and my assignment was to choose a local Target and a local Western Union to assess. The Western Union aspect made me suspicious so I wrote back saying that I changed my mind. Then I received an email saying that a Federal Express package would be arriving with money orders and instructions, money orders in the amount of $1800. I found the package on my porch and really just wanted to send it back but that would cost me money. I still have the money orders. The local police won't do anything saying that unless I was a victim of a crime, no crime has been committed. What would you do with the package?

Of course, the answer is just throw it all out. It would have been a crime – mail fraud, if the counterfeit checks had been sent via USPS and then you could have taken them the Postal Inspector. But most scammers know not to send via USPS and use services like Federal Express, which is a private company and does not follow-up on things like this.

The next scammer example must think he's from some religious order. He signs his email 'Brother Calvin'. This was a spam he sent out to probably everyone who posted a resume on Craigslist (notice the TO field). And see how he falsified the FROM email but set the REPLY-TO to his disposable email account at mail.com:

EXAMPLE EMAIL:

```
Received: from User (24.229.186.53.res-
cmts.sm.ptd.net [24.229.186.53])

(Authenticated sender:
madtexaninmaine@fairpoint.net)

Reply-To: [Shoppers_Recruitment@mail.com]

From: "S-S-N @2.0.1.2"[hostmaster@telus.net]

Subject: SECRET SHOPPER IN THE WORK 2012

Message-Id:
[20120917222717.3AE0F10412D@smtp1.av-mx.com]

To: undisclosed-recipients:;

HELLO,,,

You have been selected for assignment as a
```

Secret shopper in your area.

You will get $200 has been a Secret shopper.

Your employment packet will include funds for the shopping.

Full job description will be sent to you prior in your assignment.

You will have access to training materials after you register.

Payment check/money order would be in a certain amount

which you be required to cash your b a n k, deduct your

salary and have the rest used for evaluation.

Provide the following information if you interested and we will get back

shortly with an your assignment.

_N_a_m_e (F|L) :

_A_d_d_r_e_s_s_ :

_C_o_u_n_t_r_y_ :

_S_t_a_t_e_ :

_C_i_t_y_ :

_Z_1_P_ :

_A_G_E_:

_P_h_0_n_e_s_ :

_0_c_c_u_p_a_t_i_o_n :

_@-M_a_i_l_ :

Your response would be greatly Appreciated, Thank you.

```
Sincerely,

Brother Calvin.
```

6. **Nanny Scam**

The Nanny Scam also uses the classic check cashing scam and packages the "story" of the scam as a job opportunity. Many people selling items on Craigslist are dealing with this same check cashing scam. This is just the nanny job opportunity variation of the same thing.

How this works is a scammer will post a job opportunity for a nanny. The story may include that they live somewhere else, outside the country, but are moving to your town. The scammer will offer you the job and never even ask for your resume or do a background check. This is a big flag. And the opportunity usually includes some promise of a high wage. The next step of the scam is they will send you a check as part of a pre-payment on your salary – to show their commitment, and before you begin to buy some incidental items, which are typically toys or sometimes a wheelchair for a disabled child.

When the check arrives, the amount is for more than the expected amount, often by $1500-$5000. They will then have one of two types of stories – one will be that because they are currently out of the country, they are asking you to deposit the check and forward the "difference" to their shipping company who is handling their move, or secondly they may say their wife or assistant wrote the check out for the wrong amount by mistake and could you send the difference back to them. A critical red flag is they will *always* ask this money be sent via wire transfer, like Western Union or MoneyGram (MoneyGram recently had to pay a $100 million dollar settlement for "aiding and abetting wire fraud." Yea!).

If you continue to fall through the scam, you will deposit the check and it is likely that the bank will accept the check for deposit, but it will later turn out to be fraudulent and you are responsible for the full amount. In the meantime, you have already wired the "difference" to the scammer (there is no shipping company, by the way) via Western Union. Once the scammer picks up the money, it is untraceable and gone, as is the scammer.

7. **Medical Billing Scam**

When you see job ads for medical billing from home, you should just close the ad and move on to other opportunities. This is not really a job ad but a promotion to buy a kit to start a home business doing medical billing for doctors. The kits can be pretty pricey and there will be a sales pitch on what great money you can make and what a huge need this is for doctors. The ads will say their kit includes everything you need, including software and even a list of doctors as your beginning leads list. After you've spent thousands for such a kit, reality will set in and it will become impossible to get your money back. In the worse cases, the software does not work and the list of doctors are not leads at all, but just a list of doctors names, who have no interest in outsourcing their medical billing.

The other piece of reality about this scam is that most doctors who do outsource their medical billing do so with companies that are reputable in the industry and have a track record – not an individual working from home who has no track record and may or may not disappear without notice.

The scammer is focused on selling the kit and doesn't really care about the rest of it.

8. **Envelope Stuffing Scam**

This is actually not a job opportunity. The ad makes it seem like it is something to make extra cash by the simple task of stuffing envelopes and mailing them, but the real motive of the ad is to get you to pay for information on how to make big money stuffing envelopes. Once you pay the fee, the information either never comes or what comes is useless – usually advice to post an ad just like they did. Here is one example of what these ads might look like:

$600 to $5,000 weekly. Ten dollars for each stuffed envelope you mail...Free postage...Free circulars...No newspaper ads...No magazine ads...No bulletin board ads! Paychecks mailed to you every week! Advance paycheck forms included in your package!

The scammer doesn't have to worry about any paychecks because the scam never reaches that point. In my opinion, I do not think there is any such thing as a legitimate opportunity to be paid to stuff envelopes.

9. **Rebate Processing Scam**

This job advertisement might look like a reasonable way for someone to supplement their income. The ad will say something like you can make $500 a day processing manufacturer rebates. Once you reply to the ad, you are told you need to pay a fee for a required instructional manual on how to process the rebates. Once the money is paid, the manual never comes and the scammer is gone.

10. **Foreclosed Home Inspector Scam**

This scam will present itself as a job opportunity to inspect homes foreclosed by banks. When a job seeker replies to this ad, they are then told they need to pay a fee for liability insurance and another fee for a background check. All of that seems reasonable but once the money is paid (there will be some story as to why the money needs to be wired, which then can not be traced), the scammer is never heard from again.

Job Scam Red Flag Clues

- Any employer who is asking you for money upfront is not a legitimate employer.

- Any job opening that combines the phrases, "no experience necessary" and "earn thousands monthly" is probably a scam. Real employers ask for a resume and are seeking very specific skill sets, and don't promise that you'll make big money without having any experience.

- Any job posting that promotes "work-at-home" as its leading feature is probably a scam or MLM (Multi-Level Marketing) pyramid scheme. Legitimate jobs that can be done at home describe the job and skills sought and then at the end will mention telecommuting or home office as options.

- Job opportunities that arrive in your email, but which you did not find online and reply to, are probably not legitimate job opportunities. Employers do not proactively send out mailings to unknown candidates – they post the opening on sites like Craigslist and respond to those that reply to their posting.

- Job openings that mention "payroll assistant" or "shipping assistant" that can be done at home, from an employer who is located in a foreign country, are likely to be scams for you to reship their stolen goods and move their counterfeit checks around. Deeply research *any* employer who is located in a foreign country and is seeking work-at-home workers.

- Any employer asking for information like your social security number, credit card number or bank account numbers before you've been offered the job (okay, no employer needs to know your credit card or bank account numbers!), is probably a scammer in the process of trying to steal your identity information. Only show an employer your social security number if you are physically in their office and already have been offered and accepted a job.

- Be wary of any potential, but unfamiliar, employer who never asks for your resume.

- Be wary of employers who communicate with you through some private email instead of through the official company email. Also check that any phone number provided matches any faked letterhead they provide, and do not fax information to a fax number if you have not confirmed the destination of that fax number. Also be wary of any job opportunity that asks you to send your resume to an email address that comes from a free service, like Gmail, Hotmail, Yahoo or the such. These are almost always not real job opportunities, but a way to collect your information.

SCAM TIP:

If you are on active duty in the military, you can get an active duty alert on your credit files, good for 12 months, just to make sure no scammer applies for credit in your name.

CHAPTER 7: LINKEDIN SCAMS

LinkedIn

www.linkedin.com

With over 110 million estimated unique monthly visitors recorded in September 2012, LinkedIn is ranked number 6 for social media destination sites. The site was built to provide a professional networking platform for working people. It removes much of the daily personal "noise" of Facebook and Twitter, and focuses strictly on working people in their professional lives. But scammers love to troll for victims on this site as well.

1. Fake Contact Requests

One of the most prevalent scams on LinkedIn is the fake contact request notification email. Making professional connections on LinkedIn is the main point of using the site so scammers insert themselves into this common activity to try and trick users into their scams.

In some cases, just clicking on the link will result in either a virus getting downloaded or perhaps spyware (which silently and invisibly monitors your keystrokes looking for usernames and passwords to your accounts). In other cases, the link will redirect you to another page that still looks like it is LinkedIn (but it is not) and it will ask you to log in. Now the scammer has your password. Then it will deliver another page that presents a survey (with some incentive – job leads or more contacts or the ability to see more information about who is looking at your account) and that survey will attempt to collect even more information you should not be sharing (bank accounts, credit card numbers, social security number, etc).

Another type of fake contact request notification email is the kind that is really just an ad for some kind of pharmaceutical, either contained in a link to an external web page or contains an advertisement somewhere within the email. Related to this, some of these links go to pages of affiliate links where the scammer is paid either for each view of the ad or for any clicks on the links of that external web page. And remember, sometimes these links are "hidden" in that the part of the link you see the link looks like it is going some place innocent but when you pass your mouse over the link (without clicking on it), you will see the actual destination is an entirely different website, usually malicious or full of affiliate links.

2. Fake Job Opportunities

LinkedIn is a professional network and a place one can find job opportunities. That means scammers are going to be all over it, posting their fake and scam job openings. If you jump back to the Craigslist chapter of this book and review all the scams under the employment section, you will see examples of all of these scams on LinkedIn as well. There will be the fake applications and the "payroll assistant" for a foreign company that turns out to be a job moving counterfeit checks around, "shipping assistants" who basically receive stolen goods (a felony) and re-ship them to foreign destinations. And there are those "mystery shoppers" or "quality control specialists" who are asked to receive a check, deposit the check, and then forward a portion back to the "employer" (scammer in this case) via Western Union to test how well the service works. The check will be counterfeit, your money is good (and gone) and no one was really testing the Western Union service. They just needed the money wired because then it is untraceable and the scammer can not be tracked down and arrested.

3. Tips for Staying Safe on LinkedIn

- Do not put more personal information on LinkedIn than you absolutely need to properly use the site.

- Do not click on links in ANY email notification from LinkedIn. Open a new browser window, type in www.linkedin.com yourself, log in, and check your account from there.

- Pass your mouse over any links (without clicking) to make sure you are not being redirected to a malicious web page.

- Never pay for a job application, or pay to be "tested" before you've met with the employer face-to-face, or pay for a kit or for equipment from an unseen employer, or provide personal information like credit card numbers and social security number to an unseen employer. I'd skip the whole mystery shopper area.

- Change your password regularly and make it harder to guess by using numbers and symbols as well as upper and lower case letters.

- Do not put your email address in your profile. Keep that hidden.

CHAPTER 8: ONLINE DATING SCAMS

This topic was so important I wanted to write a separate chapter on it. Not on one specific dating site, but the scammer problem as it relates to all online dating sites. So many men and women fall victim to this scam. According to the Internet Crime Complaint Center (www.ic3.gov), in 2011, dating scams raked in $50.4 million. And a recent Glamour Magazine report claims 1 in 10 profiles on online dating sites are, in fact, scammers.

1. Dating Red Flags

I'll discuss some types of dating scams in this chapter, but from right the beginning, I wanted to start out giving you the list of warning signs in dating scams:

Scam Alert Red Flag Clues

The Profile – it's not always easy to determine if someone's profile is phoney, but look for clues such as their accomplishments which seem too good to be true, they do not seem to be able to communicate about local activities they are supposedly interested in, they can not identify particular places from a location they are supposedly from, and the photo is often lifted from other sites, including from modeling agencies. Lately, with men, they often say they are in the military or working in some capacity with the war effort. Or they have some vague government contracting job.

The Location – if the person is located overseas or says they are temporarily on assignment overseas, the odds of them being a scammer go up astronomically.

The Time Frame – for scammers, time is money. With dating scams, they will invest a lot more time "wooing" their victims than other online scams. It could be weeks, sometimes months. That's because the potential reward at the end is greater. What you will sense from a scammer is that they talk about the relationship in serious terms way too fast. They are in love with you almost immediately. They ask for your email too soon. They push to get out of the system the dating site provides and into email directly with you, or get on an instant message system or Skype (but careful if they use Skype in text mode only). They talk about having met their soul mate without having ever met you! Too soon, too fast. If your gut tells you it doesn't feel right, trust it. And if your gut is telling you they are saying everything you want to hear and they are in love but you've never met them in person, red flags are waving all over the place.

Tag Team – the money stolen in these scams is substantial and sometimes the scammer is actually a team of scammers who tag-team each other and work the scam together. If something suddenly changes about their language pattern, their use of information already shared, how they spell words, you are very likely dealing with a team of scammers.

Equal Participation – if the online communications are always dominated by you or you as a topic and they are not sharing or even seem to be withholding information – not being forthcoming. This would be a red flag for you to take a deeper look at all the other clues as well.

Secrecy – because the scammer doesn't want you talking to anyone who may figure out the relationship is a scam, the scammer will come up with some reason why the two of you should keep this wonderful growing relationship a secret. Secrecy also isolates the victim.

2. The Money Hooks

All dating scams have one main goal – money. The scammers want to trick their victims into sending them as much money as possible. These dating scams are also referred to "sweetheart scams." So let's review the main dating scam "hooks" (how scammers move their victims towards sending money):

- The scammer first spends a little time developing a relationship with the victim and tells the victim they have met the perfect person and they should get married.

- The scammer suddenly claims there is some kind of emergency in the overseas country where they are located (even if temporarily) and need of the victim's help financially.

-The scammer unexpectedly claims a medical emergency and needs money.

- The scammer needs help with travel expenses or to pay off recent credit card debt ("I'll pay you back, sweetheart." No, they won't.)

- The scammer may say they have immigration problems and need money so they can come visit the victim.

- The scammer asks if they can send the victim a check and asks the victim to deposit the check and send a portion of the money on to their mother or uncle or some family member or business associate, via wire transfer. This is *always* a scam. The original check will turn out to be counterfeit but your money is good, and gone.

- And in a final twist the knife in the gut move, if a scammer suspects the victim is on to him/her, they may have someone call the victim pretending to be the police and asking for a fee to be paid to have the scammer arrested. No one will be arrested. It is still a scam.

Remember, the money portion of the scam can begin at any time – some scammers woo their victims for months while others move more quickly. Your job, to avoid being a victim, is to decide – firmly and with no exceptions, that you are not going to send money to anyone whom you have not met face-to-face. And even then, I would say just don't do it - period. But that's my comfort level with this issue. You'll have to decide your comfort level in your face-to-face dating relationships. I'd make sure you know their parents and siblings and cousins and aunts and uncles and neighbors and check to see if you still feel comfortable giving that person money. A small bit of money – no problem. A larger loan – think long and hard. And then some.

3. Other Dating Schemes

Blackmail Scam

This scam typically involves a woman in cooperation with a male scammer. The woman will target connecting with men on online dating sites – any of them will do. She will chat up the victim for awhile, until she thinks the male victim is "warmed up" and then offer something very few men refuse – she offers to strip for him via webcam. She does and then asks him to reciprocate. When he does, the scam has now moved to the critical stage. Very soon after the victim has stripped for the webcam, he will receive an email that says something like, "Have a look at this video I've taken of you. I am going to put it on YouTube unless you send me some money in order to not make it available online." The video will show the victim's face and everything. One victim refused and his video was posted to gay pornography websites. Other scammers, in order to apply more pressure, will use the tactic of setting up fake websites to make it look like they are the police or Interpol and accuse the victim of pornography and stripping before a minor, then demand a "fine." This is an effective scam because the victims are typically so ashamed of their behavior that they are not going to report it and will pay the fine to make it go away.

Fake Phone Number Scam

Someone has contacted you online, given you a phone number to call them and you do, only to find out later it was linked to a 900 number and you have a huge phone bill. My advice? Try and do a reverse phone lookup on any number you are given and see if it makes sense with all the other information they are providing you. Even if there is a fee to find that out, it's worth it.

Prostitute Scammers

Prostitutes love to frequent the online dating sites and

pretend to be trolling for dates but "dates" has a very different meaning to them – it's business and it is going to cost you. Their profiles and photos are often sleazy enough that you can kind of tell, but be careful of the prostitute – male or female, on the prowl.

4. Dating Stories

Many people think, "I'd never do that!", but shockingly many intelligent regular people fall for dating scams. These scams work because scammers target emotional vulnerabilities. And we all know cases where perfectly intelligent people have done really dumb things for love. Let's review a few real-life stories and see if you can identify the patterns scammers use.

Story 1

"Karen" is a 73-year-old widow of eight years when she felt like she wanted companionship and love again. She went on the dating site called PlentyOfFish.com to look for possible companions. She exchanged messages with a few men that didn't seem her type but she was intrigued by one man, Don, who said he was a 66-year-old American of Swedish descent who was raised in California and currently working overseas as an oil procurement specialist (what makes a scammer good at what they do is that the victim will often say later that the scammer knew exactly the perfect things to say and how to appeal exactly to what they were seeking in a relationship).

They conversed online for about 6-8 weeks and things were going really well until Don ran into some unexpected situations with his work. The first situation was that Don said an important client of his couldn't pay him because he was not able to send the money internationally. He asked Karen, just in the short term, if she could loan him the money until he could collect from his client and then he would pay her back. Karen felt they had built up a lot of trust and intimacy over the weeks and she wired him the money.

A week later, Karen received a call from Don who was at the hospital. He explained to Karen that he didn't have the money to pay his hospital bill because that important client still hadn't paid him. He even got the doctor (who was just another scammer) on the phone to explain Don's medical procedures. Don promised to pay her back. Karen wired the money.

Six months later, it could now be tallied up that Karen had sent Don more than $100,000 and she realized something was not right and she might not get her money back. She went to the authorities who were not able to recoup any money but they did find out that Don was really a Nigerian living in London and had assumed the identity of a real man from California.

Story 2

This woman met her man at an online dating "event" for Christians. They had quickly moved their communications to Facebook, then to Yahoo Messenger, and then to the telephone. They had been speaking almost every day for about 2 months but had never met face-to-face.

The woman believed they fell in love and that they were going to get married. He said he was a traveling salesman and on the road a lot. At one point he asked her to help him out with some supplies from other countries and he would share his profits with her for helping him out.

He sent her money order checks totalling $20,000. He then asked her to send $4500 to a different person who had supplies for him, via Western Union. She went to the bank and deposited the checks and placed the order with Western Union. She became suspicious, went back to the bank and found out the checks were counterfeit. She cancelled the Western Union order in time (which you can do if the scammer has not already picked up the money; they know this, so they do everything they can to get the money order picked up as quickly as possible and disappear).

This story had a lucky ending.

Story 3

A 32-year-old disabled man who had some learning disabilities and was partially deaf was approached by a gang of scammers posing as a glamorous female, Lydia. Lydia first reached out to this man on Facebook and then quickly moved their communications to MSN Messenger (scammers do this because it is harder for authorities to get information on their activities than if they stayed on Facebook). They conversed for about 8 weeks and this man thought Lydia was going to come to the UK so they could get married. He wired her money for travel expenses and spending money. Then "she" asked for wedding expenses, including the dress, the cake, and jewelry. All of this took place without the man's parents or sister knowing anything about it.

When she didn't arrive, he got a call from a doctor (just another scammer in the gang) who said she had been in a plane accident on her way to London. He wired money for her medical expenses. When she recovered, he wired one more round of travel expenses. Then she said if money was wired to a Platinum Trust Security Bank he would get a share of her $500,000 inheritance. Finally, they sensed they were almost done bleeding this guy dry, so "she" said she would turn him over to the police for illegally purchasing a woman online if he didn't keep sending her payments to keep quiet. He went to the bank to take out two loans and extend his overdraft protection. That is when it finally got someone's attention. Total loss? $50,000.

Story 4

A woman in her late 60's met someone on a dating site who said he was working at the London Olympics (obviously, this scam went on while the London Olympics were taking place, but you can apply this scam any time a worldwide known event is taking place). She tried to take $80,000 from her bank to send to him but the bank refused to wire the money. Good for the bank! The scammer made two mistakes – he went for too much money in one round and he didn't make sure his victim used Western Union and not their bank – the bank would know better, and *did* know better.

The bank contacted the Department of Public Safety in their state and a representative called the woman and explained the scheme to her. But she didn't believe the agent and without their knowledge, she went to another bank where she had an account and wired the money (shame on that bank for allowing such a transfer). She then left the country and went to London to meet her man. Which, to no surprise, she was not able to find. The authorities were eventually able to catch the scammers who turned out to be a 19-year-old Nigerian man and an Argentine woman pretending to be a dapper older gentleman. No money was recovered.

Story 5

George met his online scammer who claimed she was a 35-year-old woman from Ghana named "Liz," who worked in accounting and loved sports. She provided him with lots of photographs. She asked him for help within days of beginning their online relationship. The amount was small, $200, and the reason seemed understandable.

Then it just became one problem after another, she needed money to fix each one. There would be weeks of silence and then she would return again with another problem and another request for money. George would say he never thought he could be manipulated the way he was, but in the end it turned out he could be.

George's suspicions got more serious when he sent travel expenses but she never showed up for Christmas. Because of his uncertainties, he stopped talking about his online relationship to his family and friends but he did continue to send her money.

"You get into a habit and after awhile I felt every day there was going to be a new request." Some requests were as small as $50 and other requests were larger. The largest wire transfer was $10,000 over two days, which would cover her coming to live with him for 3 months.

Total loss? $40,000.

George has some advice for other people considering sending money overseas: even if there is only 1% of doubt, trust your gut, and do not proceed. You will never see that money again.

SCAM TIP:

If someone contacts you saying you've been a victim of fraud, do NOT give out ANY personal information until you can verify the person's identity through some other objective source. Do NOT wire money to any person for any reason, even if the person says they are with the FBI.

CHAPTER 9: ADDITIONAL SCAMS

1. Flickr Scams

Flickr is an online photo management and sharing network, one that preceded Pinterest. In September 2012, it was estimated that Flickr had 90 million unique monthly visitors. That's a lot of people, and sure to attract the scammers. Here are some of the more common things to watch out for:

Phishing Emails

These take two main forms – the first are emails saying the sender has a question about your photo on Flickr. But the link in the email goes to a fake page, typically to get your login and more information via a survey.

Secondly, these phishing emails might just be a user (who turns out to be a scammer) asking if you will help them with their research, but the research is just a survey to collect as much personal information on you as they can, regardless of how confidential they say the results will be.

Comment Scams

Comments can be within groups or under photos. Scammers love to leave messages that have links in them redirecting the user to fake pages that look like Flickr but ask the user to log in to continue. And then the scammer has access to that account or there may be a collection of photos of a topic you like but when you click on that collection, you end up on a site outside of Flickr (but may not notice it because it looks just like Flickr) and again, it will ask you to log in to continue. Scammers will use your account to send messages to other people, post comments with malicious links and other nefarious things.

Tips for Staying Safe on Flickr

Don't click on any links in emails, comments or groups without passing your mouse over them first (without clicking) and seeing if the actual destination matches where the links say they are going.

Don't ever log in from a link in an email or if prompted on a web page after clicking on a link in an email. Open a new browser window, type in www.flickr.com yourself, and log in from there.

2. MySpace Scams

With over 70.5 million unique monthly visitors estimated in September 2012, despite its history, MySpace remains amongst the top ranking social media destinations.

In June 2011, Specific Media Group and Justin Timberlake purchased MySpace for $35 million dollars. In late September, early October 2012, press started appearing that a completely overhauled and newly designed MySpace was about to be re-launched. It's not the first time the site has tried to "re-boot" since losing its market to Facebook, but owners are pitching this re-launch as a return to its original focus – a social network for musicians, artists, and celebrities with an interface that is very visual, has similarities to Pinterest, but scrolls horizontally instead of vertically. It will be interesting to see, as Facebook's "cool" factor begins to wane, if a re-vamped MySpace can become a Facebook alternative. Also, returning to its niche as a social network for musicians, actors, artists might work in the same way that LinkedIn works as a niched social network for working professionals. It remains to be seen where musicians and celebrities will go to hang out and where their fans want to hang out.

MySpace has not yet officially been re-launched as of the writing of this book. So if you want to be scam-prepared, re-read the chapters on Facebook (because MySpace will have many Facebook-like features), YouTube (because MySpace will have many video clips and places to put comments), and sections on Pinterest and Flickr (because MySpace will also be very visual and have photo sharing and comments for that as well).

3. Google+ Scams

With 65 million unique monthly visitors estimated in September 2012, Google+ is a top social media network contender and was launched as a competing service to Facebook. As mentioned earlier in this book, this site is a late entry for Google. It still remains to be seen how well the market will adapt to it and if it can compete with Facebook. I have seen a fan base of people there who have abandoned Facebook and love Google+. I have an account on Google+ and tried it for a little while. But wasn't able to take to it, mostly because, for me, very few people I knew or wanted to connect with, were using it. But who knows what will happen over time. More recently, a colleague has been hosting video "hangouts" on Google+ so I have been checking it out again. If you can count on anything with the Internet, it is that things will change and evolve.

When Google+ started, it was by invitation only. The scammers jumped on this and began sending out fake emails that looked like real Google+ invitations, but actually the invitation link in the email landed the user on a page that downloaded a virus. This fake invitation to Google+ spread all over Facebook in 2011. Pinterest had the same problem when it launched in an invite-only mode. But both platforms, Google+ and Pinterest, are fully open now so that particular problem has gone away. But any new service that crops up and has an initial period of invitation only, users should watch out for those bogus invitations.

Because Google+ is like Facebook in many ways, you'll be prepared for the scams that occur on Google+ by re-reading the chapter on Facebook scams. All the same types of links which redirect you to pages that advertise pharmaceuticals or have affiliate links. All the same tricks. So re-read the Facebook chapter and you should be well armed to deal with scams on Google+.

4. Tumblr Scams

With 26 million unique monthly visitors estimated for September 2012, Tumblr is a micro-blogging website similar to Twitter but with a more visual and multimedia bent to it. Twitter launched in the summer of 2006 and

Tumblr launched in the spring of 2007. Tumblr has a respectable audience size but did not garner the popularity and branding of Twitter. It is Twitter's smaller, younger cousin. Okay, all you Tumblr fans, shoot me now for saying that. But because these services are similar in many ways, I'd consider the scams on Tumblr probably to be very similar to what you'd find on Twitter.

For example, watch out for spam messages coming via your "Ask Boxes" referring to TumblrDating.com or TumblrTasks.com – with incentives to click on the links. Refrain from clicking on a link because you just get redirected to advertising pages with affiliate links or to pages to trick you into signing up for services that will, in the end, have monthly charges attached. Also watch out for requests to re-blog hot newsworthy items like earthquake events or any natural disasters. You can choose to re-blog something, but when someone requests you to do this, skip it. And finally, because there are a lot of younger people on Tumblr, the site has more scams whenever a new software or video game is released, which contain messages claiming to have a free copy to offer or the secrets for defeating the game.

5. DeviantArt Scams

DeviantArt is an online community devoted to visual artists and, as such, it attracts scammers because artists can be a vulnerable group (I know – I am an artist). With 25.1 million monthly visitors estimated in September 2012, DeviantArt has enough of an audience to attract the scammers.

Many of the scams you'll see on DeviantArt are similar to other sites – scammers will create fake login pages in order to try and steal passwords. Once they hack into an account, they can begin sending spam to other members and posting public messages with malicious links.

But of course, my favorite one – the one that gets my blood boiling, is when scammers come to DeviantArt (and to any artist) and pretend to want to buy their artwork, only to overpay with a counterfeit check and trick the artist into forwarding their own good money on to a non-existent shipper via Western Union, thinking they have the buyer's money covered in the bank. And then the bank takes the money back because it is fraudulent and the artist is left on the hook. "Starving artists" is a phrase that was coined for a reason. Lots of artists are living on the financial edge in order to create their work. That scammers will go after the little money that artists do have, just makes me insane. It is why I started my blog, StopArtScams, my Facebook page, and this series of books. I got tired of receiving emails from heartbroken artists who had just lost a couple thousand dollars to a scammer. Not only was it the lost money, but artists can feel heartbroken that someone didn't love their painting after all or that the painting they loved got shipped to god-knows-where and can not be recovered.

6. Digg Scams

Digg is a web content sharing social media site. Users can vote articles and other content up or down (called digging or burying) to share with others. With 25.1 million unique visitors estimated in September 2012, Digg has an audience and scammers are not going to ignore this.

If the site is based on voting to increase or decrease the visibility of someone's content on the web, you've just established a black market for buying votes in order to increase the visibility of the content you own. The site may have affiliate links or some other means of generating revenue for you, or at least some system of voter fraud. Digg has been struggling with this issue of voting fraud throughout its existence. Given this possibility, if a page has a lot of votes, I would not necessarily believe it is important, nor would I believe (without checking other independent sources) that it is legitimate and safe.

There are also scams of fake or duplicate content itself rising to higher visibility in order to get you to click on links on that page, which then try to get you to give up your login information and any other information.

7. Pinterest Scams

Pinterest is pretty far down this list but I'm confident it won't stay there long. Pinterest has grown 866% just over the last year so I expect to see this site rise even further in prominence in a very short time. As of September 2012, Pinterest has an estimated 23 million monthly unique users.

With all the attention being showered on photo "pin-up" website Pinterest lately, it was inevitable that criminals would figure out a way to cash in on this popular social-media site. New point-and-click software available in underground markets attract criminals/scammers by helping even the most technically unsophisticated people to prey on the gullibility of other users. A couple of readily available toolkits allow scammers to earn fraudulent referral fees - from Amazon, online survey services, and premium telephone numbers.

The scams work by the scammer posting a photo and in the caption putting some great offer and a link, getting people to re-pin it, and redirecting unwitting Pinterest users to links they didn't intend on visiting. In the case of one popular pin advertising a coffee chain, the deal prompted the user to plug the product on Facebook and install some software before asking for private information.

Other scams on Pinterest feature suspicious lines like "OMG I have just received this gift card, get one here!" and prompts users to re-pin the ad in order to take advantage of the offer. Resist the temptation, fellow pinners. Before you re-pin that alluring free makeup deal, ask yourself: "Does this image look like something that actually came from the brand, or does it look amateurish?" "Does the brand's logo look strange?" "What about the text?" If the art looks like it was put together by some amateur, move on. Do not give out your personal information - even if they offer a free car... maybe *especially* if they offer a free car.

Pinterest also experiences what is known as "paraody accounts" where people set up accounts under the name of famous people - celebrities or political figures. These are typically taken down once identified to the site, but more continually pop up.

8. LiveJournal Scams

LiveJournal was an early entry to the social media landscape, launched in 1999 as a place where people could keep their journals online (a concept that eventually evolved into blogs). By September of 2012, LiveJournal's unique monthly visitor audience was estimated to be 20.5 million. Its social media aspects include being able to "friend" other people's journals so their entries show up for you, as well as the ability to comment on entries.

The scams on this site are related to any scams you would find on a blogging service, typically via the comments sections. Scammers love to post comments that pretend to be engaged in your posting but are not, and then include a link to their Viagra page or what-have-you. Scammers will use the comment section to bring attention to some great survey for you to fill out or a free gift card offer you can't miss. You need to delete these from your own comments section and not click on those links when you see them in the comments section of other people's livejournals. Scammers are all trying to re-direct you to advertisements or collect your personal information. So don't do it.

9. Tagged Scams

Tagged calls itself a "social discovery" site, allowing users to meet and socialize with new people through shared interests, games, suggestions from friends, etc. With 19.5 million estimated unique visitors, as of September 2012, Tagged has its share of scams, as any social site will. Here are some to be on the watch for:

Tagged Lottery – some scams purport to say you've won a lottery or contest hosted by Tagged. This is never the case and it is in your interest to just delete those messages.

Fake Administrative Messages – this has been seen on other sites as well, messages that look like they are from Tagged saying they've run out of disk space (or some other terrible site-wide catastrophe) and you need to reply to the email to verify your identity so that your account will not be deleted. It's a fake and the scammer will try and collect your login information as well as any other personal information they can.

Fake Check Scam – this is the usual scam where the scammer sends a check, asks you to deposit it and send a portion elsewhere via a wire transfer. Their check is counterfeit, and your money is good and long gone.

Fake Friends – this is where some girl (or guy) reaches

out to you and immediately tries to switch you to communicating outside the system – via Yahoo or MSN Messenger, or Skype (in text mode), or just their email which will also be from a free web email source. These "friends" are scammers trolling for victims. Also be very wary of *any* person you just met on Tagged (or anywhere online) who begins asking for money – for any set-up emergency or sob-story reason. These are scammers.

10. Etsy Scams

Etsy was launched in June 2005, an e-commerce website focused on handmade or vintage items as well as art and craft supplies. I'm fond of Etsy. I've been on Etsy for many years. I love the idea of a site focused on handmade items by the artisans themselves. It's slowly changing focus from its original vision but for right now, remains an active website for handcrafted items.

Etsy is not an auction site. It is a fixed-listing selling platform. They have a "community" where buyers and sellers can participate in forums. Although scammers have a harder time penetrating Etsy, they have definitely made their presence known. For example, it is common for scammers to sign up on weekends with fake accounts and post fake (or even real, but definitely not handmade) listings. Or they start ripping through the forums with spam postings with links to their scam sites, knowing that the Etsy staff for monitoring such problems is lighter on the weekends.

Fake Etsy Buyer Scam

I've started receiving emails from Etsy sellers stating that scammers are pulling the common Fake Buyer Scam, pretending to want to buy their product but writing to sellers with some fake story about how they can't use PayPal and would prefer to send a check and they have a shipper who can pick everything up. And you guessed it, eventually they will send a money order check for over the amount and ask the seller to send the difference on to the buyer's shipper, via wire transfer. They hope the seller will do this before they figure out the original check is counterfeit and the bank takes the money back out of the seller's account. Recently, many sellers were reporting the same scammer on Etsy doing this and Etsy would shut down their account only to have this person appear again under another account. Scammers are like cockroaches, kind of hard to get rid of once you have an infestation.

My advice to Etsy sellers, to stay safe, is to keep your transactions within Etsy. Do not agree to a money order check or even a credit card outside the Etsy system. Keep with either PayPal or the Direct Pay Etsy service. And NEVER ever use a wire transfer service in your online dealings and you'll be a lot safer doing your business on Etsy. Buyers may have stories and sellers want to go out of their way to keep customers happy, but stay within the Etsy system.

SCAM TIP:

If someone calls claiming to be from the Social Security Administration (SSA) and asks for your bank account, credit card, or life insurance policy numbers, it's a scam. Hang up without saying another word.

CHAPTER 10: SECURITY & SOCIAL MEDIA

A. Social Media Assumptions

I know this is going to sound cynical or a little negative – and I definitely do not want to minimize or undercut all the great and wonderful benefits of social networking online, but in terms of security and safety, I have to address the dark side. I do this so you do not dismiss, rationalize, or deny it. The truth of the matter is that normal rules and expectations of social interactions do not apply online. I see people make some deadly assumptions:

People are telling me the truth.

People have goodwill and will not harm me.

People are who they say they are.

I can correct that person's misconception.

People are transparent online.

My friends online are trustworthy.

Smartphones are virus-free.

Everyone understands what I am saying.

Everyone finds my jokes funny.

Public wifi connections are safe.

Every online job posting represents a real job opportunity.

If I send a message to someone, they will receive and read it.

The FROM field in an email always shows where an email comes from.

People are just like me.

People like me.

People can not see information I don't want them to see.

I have a private account so I know who sees my information.

I can win a lottery I've never entered.

They will keep my credit card and social security number safe.

B. Tips to Reduce Social Media Risks

Scammers will always be seeking victims wherever people gather online. They will always be trolling the social networking websites. Here are some things you can do to reduce your scam risk while making use of social networking websites.

Privacy Settings

The biggest investment in time you can make when spending it online is to examine your privacy settings, what privacy you have, and more importantly, what privacy you do not have. It is not good enough to accept the default settings and to never look. You have to look and you have to customize your settings to your comfort level. Every social networking site has a place to review and customize privacy settings, typically found under your account settings. Also search for any opt-out links of sites following you around the internet in order to deliver you targeted ads. You may have to search in Google for these tracking settings. Not all sites even allow you to opt out, but some do and you should find them and opt out.

Your Social Network

It is not always wise to build up your "friends" list (or followers or whatever they are called on a given site) to a high number regardless of knowing them. Although there is something to be said for "audience building," having 1,000,000 friends is not a sustainable list; probably has a high percentage of faked profiles on it, and leaves you more open to scammers getting on your list and targeting you. Better to really hone your list of friends to your offline friends, family and those within your immediate and strongest interest areas. And then only grow your list organically.

I have varied interests, and so on Facebook and Twitter, I use lists to categorize my friends or people I'm following. Then I can check in on my list of artists I follow, or my list of authors, or my list of technology personalities, or my family or my local friends. Anything above that number is hard for me to track. I do scroll down my Facebook and Twitter feeds several times throughout my day, as I'm working online, and I'll see posts I don't typically see, but it's pretty hit-and-miss.

Don't go for numbers, go for quality.

Social Content You Post

In the excitement of sharing and seeing people post comments on your posts, photos and videos, people often get lulled into a sense of security and privacy (this is particularly true for young people but really I see it for any age bracket). At some point people suddenly post things that are not entirely appropriate for public consumption, one thing they do not understand, is that once content is posted online, it is never really gone, even if they delete it. It is not gone. And likely 20 years from now it will still not be gone. Did you just post something of yourself you wouldn't want to see 20 years from now, and have it come back to haunt you? Then don't post that now.

Untag your name on photos and content when you do not want to be tagged, and do not tag yourself unless you wouldn't mind that tag being there 20 years from now.

The worst example I saw, related to safety and scammers, was when there was a period of time when young people were posting photos of their brand new credit cards on their Facebook page. Egads! A field day for scammers. And those photos of you drunk and having fun at a party are not going to go over well with a current or future employer. I also wouldn't write about all the expensive things you own or readily announce you are on vacation and away from your home.

Be mindful of the content you post online.

Requests for Your Personal Information

This is a sweet spot for scammers. I think too many sites ask for too much information they don't actually need. It's data collection, it's a revenue stream to sell this data, and it's privacy invasion. It's not good. So scammers have moved into this common activity and send out emails or create fake login pages and try to collect as much personal information as they can – to steal your identity, to open credit cards, to raid your PayPal or bank account, etc.

The minute some site or email asks you to log in again or fill out information in order to validate who you are – you have to stop yourself and think real hard about why you are giving up that information, if they have a right to ask for it, and are you checking and double checking to make sure it is not a scammer faking those emails or web pages. An employer writing to you from an online job does not need to know your credit card number, or your social security number before you've met. A survey to win a prize does not need to collect your bank account or PayPal login. NO ONE online should need to know your social security number. If your online banking is asking for your social security number, close the email and get on the phone. In fact, if anyone is asking for personal information you feel you shouldn't be providing online, get on the phone instead. No one is going to think less of you if you explain that you do not give out that information online. It's also okay to call a company and ask if they sent an email asking for particular information. If it's a scam, they'll be able to confirm that for you.

Unidentifiable Links

This is one of the main ways scammers trick people into landing on web pages that are bogus and there to collect your information: login passwords, bank accounts, social and security numbers. Other reasons why scammers want you to click on their links is to download a virus or spyware (software that silently and invisibly sits on your computer and monitors all your keystrokes). Links in email, Direct Messages, on Facebook walls, in Tweets, in the comments sections of blogs and YouTube, in advertising on Craigslist – be very careful about these. Do NOT click unless you are confident of where you'll land and who is behind the link. Don't click on links that just do not seem right. There are two main types of tricky links:

Hidden Destinations – you'll see one thing in the link, but if you put your mouse over the link without clicking on it, towards the bottom of your screen, you may see a completely different URL destination in the status bar. Scammers do this on purpose because most users do not bother to even check.

Shortened URLs – these are links that are shortened by services like Bit.ly and TinyURL.com and are most often seen on Twitter because of the limitation of the posts but the links can be seen in other places and in email. You can not immediately see the destination of a shortened URL so it is not wise to test where it goes by clicking on it. By then it might be too late. Before clicking on anything, make use of one of the services that show you the original URL that's been shortened. Some examples of those services are: longurl.org, longurlplease.com, and Bing.It. You can search online for other similar services.

Online Financial Transactions

The internet is a great place to do business but it is also can be a scary place to do business. Business owners can avoid scams by keeping some basics in mind:

- never accept overpayments

- never use wire transfers

- don't accept money orders or cashier checks from anyone claiming to be moving or temporarily located overseas or out of the country

- do not give your money to anyone for housing until you've inspected the inside of the place personally and met the landlord personally

- do not pay an upfront fee to do a work-at-home job or to be tested for a job opportunity

Public Computers

It is convenient to jump on the internet at the library or other public computers but the connections are NOT safe. It is possible for another person sitting right in the same room as you to have software on their computer that allows them to grab information from your connection to the internet, including your passwords and other sensitive information. Also, do not send any emails or do any work online at a public computer that has financially-sensitive information.

Passwords

Passwords are an area which everyone needs to get a little better. We tend to make passwords too easy to guess and use one password across everything we do online. This is making it easy for scammers to break into accounts and send out spam.

My advice to make your passwords more complicated and use some system offline (not on your computer) to keep track of all of them (I know, that won't help if you've taped it to the wall next to the computer and a burglar breaks in, but hey, I'm not trying to cover *every* scenario). Use upper and lowercase letters, some numbers and a symbol some place in your password. And change it once in awhile.

Security Software

Always make sure your typical virus protection and firewall software is up to date. Battling viruses and spyware and is an ongoing battle. They are called viruses for very good reason – they keep changing, evolving, adapting and avoiding detection. Your virus protection software has a database that keeps track of all the latest versions of viruses and, to be useful to you, this database must be kept very up to date to be useful to you.

Mobile Technology (smart phones, tablets cell phones, etc)

Smartphones, tablets and other mobile technologies are not immune to scams, viruses, and spyware. It is not as common – yet – but viruses on mobile devices is inevitable and already starting to appear. Do not be lulled into a false sense of security just because you are on your smartphone.

Javelin Strategy and Research released a study that demonstrates the risk mobile users create. This study, reflecting 2011 numbers, showed 7% of cellphone users were victims of Identity Theft; 62% said they don't use a password on their cellphone and 32% said they were saving their logins right on the cellphone; 68% shared their birthday online, and 45% included the year; 63% shared their high school name; 18% shared their phone number; and 12% shared a pet's name. Hmmm, maybe I can break into your bank account.

Your cellphone, ipad or tablet is not safe. Treat each as if they are a little computer and use the same safety measures you would on your computer. These devices *are* becoming your computer.

You will begin to see scammers target smartphones and tablets with more frequency. But much of what I've already talked about in this book applies to your mobile technology. Extend your safety measures to your mobile devices. Don't leave the back door open to scammers.

Educate Your Children

Kids take to technology much more easily than older people. They are thriving with social media and mobile technology. But they are still kids and parents need to support them in reducing their risks:

- You must have a candid conversation with them, periodically, about who they are interacting with electronically and how (i.e. texting, photos, etc). If they are under-age, parents should insist on password access to all their accounts.

- Have your child use a first name only or nickname, not their full first and last name.

- Educate yourself as a parent about any social media sites your children are using and make sure their privacy settings have been properly customized.

- Be aware of how easy it is to geo-locate your children through their mobile devices. There is a benefit for you, but make sure that not just anyone can locate your children.

- Insist that, without an adult present, your child NEVER meet anyone in person they've only known online.

- Have a candid conversation with your child about what they can do when their "creep meter" goes off.

- Have that important conversation how talking about sex online, even on their mobile devices, is the most dangerous thing they can do when they are online. Sharing photos that are sexually explicit – even to each other, is actually illegal if the child is under-age. Parents can be held legally liable. Children need to understand they are not private and safe when they are texting or using social media online.

- Have a conversation about cyber-bullying, what behavior is considered cyberbullying, what the risks are legally, and what steps they can take if they feel someone is cyberbullying them.

- Tell your child you will not monitor every word but will be doing random spot checks on what they are saying, what kind of photos they are sending or receiving, and with whom they are interacting.

- Don't be afraid to take away your child's account if he or she does not abide by your rules – your child may not be ready for online independence. You can always revisit the topic when your child shows that they are more ready.

SCAM TIP:

Do not use software that auto-fills your passwords, account numbers, and credit card numbers – these make it easy for scammers who get access to your computer to easily find this information.

CONCLUSION

The world is getting more connected every day. Web 1.0 was about static content and easy access to a ton of information via fast searches. Web 2.0 pushes static content to the background in favor of interactive communities and user-generated content. It appears that users have shifted from static authority-based information to moving, interactive information "streams," where anyone can contribute. And the stream is only getting more fluid as technology moves further away from the desktop towards mobile gadgets.

I love social media. I love hearing what people are thinking, even if I don't agree with them. I love seeing a stream of human expression – of thoughts, feelings, images - the flow of people's lives. I love seeing the diversity and complexity and how this is reflected online as people connect with one another and share.

The good news is that anyone can say anything. And the bad news is anyone can say anything. This is a double-edged sword. It is both a higher level of freedom, a higher level of access to information, as well as a higher level of individual responsibility. The previous barriers and screening of information have given way to anyone saying anything. On the other side of this coin, in this new environment, users have a greater responsibility to use their discernment in order to determine what is true and what is not, what is useful to their lives and what is not.

And it is human nature that whenever a great thing makes enormous advances, the dark side reacts and wants to re-assert its presence. Whenever freedom makes an advance, fear stands up and screams louder, like a child having a tantrum. The totality of our human experience is both light and dark and this is certainly reflected online in social media. So while we experience all the benefits of social media, we must also be prepared to handle the darker aspects of the experience. That includes arming yourself with information about how to avoid becoming a victim of a scammer. Knowledge is power in this case. Know what scammers are doing, know how to recognize a scam in the social media environment, and know how to avoid their traps.

Protect your information, know what you are posting online, understand who can see what you are posting online, do not believe everything you are told online (check out information through other objective sources), do not click on links until you absolutely understand where you are being redirected to, do not cash checks for people and then forward money elsewhere, never use wire transfers (I know that sounds extreme but that's how I feel – scammers *need* wire transfers to steal money and not be traceable), do not give out your personal information to people you do not know, understand that scammers are not going away and are going to keep adapting (much like cockroaches), and do not believe you are in love with someone you have never met face-to-face. And no, you did not win a lottery you have not entered.

Enjoy social media – there is much to learn and experience from it. But you will be able to enjoy it with even more confidence if you are armed with the knowledge of how to recognize and avoid scammers.

GLOSSARY OF SOCIAL MEDIA TERMS

@

@

Used in an email address, @ is now also important in Twitter, as the symbol before a user's "handle" or username. When people track their interactions, using @[twitterusername] in your twitter message, they will see that message on their "connect" page and know you mentioned them specifically in your twitter message.

A

Anonoblog

A blog that is created and maintained by a person who does not reveal their identity.

API

Short for Application Programming Interface. It is how certain sites allow third-party companies to have access to their data and develop "apps" that enhance the user's experience. For example, Twitter offers a way to access their data stream through an API and as a result many companies have developed Twitter applications – to manage your postings and keep track of popular people or see who has unfollowed you.

App

App is shortened for Application and is the term used to refer to software applications written specifically to run on mobile phones. The term originally became popular with the iPhones and apps written to work on the iPhone. Now the term is gaining broader use and also refers to software applications made to work with different social media websites. For example, Facebook has a list of "apps" that once you choose to install any of them, they are made to run with Facebook and make your experience there more interesting and more useful.

AstroTurfing

This is when a person or group of people are paid to make it appear like a grassroots "buzz" has been generated around something. Often applied to political activities or corporations who generate buzz about their product rather than that buzz being generated organically by users themselves.

Avatar

Avatars are little graphical images users have in their social media account profiles instead of a photograph of themselves. Avatars began in the gaming world when an entire character of the user's choosing in the game came to represent them as a user in that game.

B

Back Channel

This is the term used when users communicate with each other through the private messaging options on different social media platforms, as opposed to posting their communications publicly.

Blog

Online diaries or journals were referred to as "weblogs" until Peter Merholz, in 1999, as a joke, broke apart the word 'weblog' on his online journal sidebar into 'we blog' and this morphed into the term we use today. Blogs continue to be online journals, with images and links, that are displayed in reverse chronological order. A blogger is a person who maintains a blog. Blog is also used now as a verb, as in "I am going to blog that when I get home."

Blogosphere

A term to describe the universe of people who use blogs and the posts that happen within that social media platform. Twitterverse is the universe that refers to Twitter users and their posts.

Blogroll

This refers to a list of other recommended blogs displayed on someone's blog.

Blog Storm

This happens when many bloggers collude (or not) to write many blog entries on a given subject and the sheer number of posts force it higher in the search results and typically into main stream media monitoring for trends and stories.

C

Cloud Computing

This is a broad term used to refer to services delivered over the Internet instead of needing a private or dedicated server., a user needs only a computer and an Internet connection to access all their files. Referred to as being in a "cloud," their music and other services, and they can access these services from anywhere. It is pretty much a reworking of the very old idea of a mainframe holding the information and users using a terminal to access the information, except there is no dedicated mainframe computer – the information is distributed and maintained by resources on the Internet. A user can also use as many or as little of the services they need, and instead of paying monthly flat fees, the fees are typically based on actual usage.

Community

Any gathering of people online with a common interest of a person, a product or brand, a topic, a hobby or profession, or in broader terms – a website (i.e. the Facebook community). Pssst – scammers are attracted to online communities like bees to nectar.

Content Management System (CMS)

These are software platforms where a front-end has been programmed to allow non-technical users to generate their own websites, blogs, online communities, etc. Wordpress is an example of a CMS system that allows users to create and maintain their own blog.

Crowdsource

This is the act of turning to social media audiences to poll for their opinion on a question. Also can be the act of posting alternative content to social media audiences and seeing which one they respond to more. It can be as simple as one person turning to their Facebook page and asking all their "friends" which smartphone should they buy or what should they have for dinner to companies polling their online audiences for user preferences and feedback.

D

Dashboard

This is the term for the main administration web page on a CMS (Content Management System), where the administrator of a website or blog can create and maintain the content on their site. Blogger.com has a dashboard from where users can create their posts, change the look of the blog, moderate comments, etc. Wordpress also has a dashboard as to many other CMS services.

Delicious

Founded in 2003 as a bookmarking service – to maintain your list of bookmarks and access them from anywhere. This service was purchased from Yahoo in 2011 by AVOS, a company by YouTube founders Chad Hurley and Steve Chen. The focus of the site, re-launched on September 2011, shifted from bookmarking to curating collections of bookmarks and discovering interesting and new links to bookmark.

Direct Message (DM)

A direct message refers to a private message sent in the Twitter system from one user to another. Only the person sending and receiving the DM message can see it. A user must be "following" the user they want to send a direct message to. Receivers of direct messages can block spammers and report them as well.

Dooced

This is when someone has been fired from their job as a result of something they posted online.

E

Ebook

Ebook is short for electronic book, which are books that have been formatted into digital files that can be read on the computer or a special "reader" for digital files. Ebooks began as PDF files that could be read by anyone with the free Adobe Reader software. Amazon created a proprietary reader called the "Kindle" which accepts MOBI format files (there is a way to convert these files from other formats). Most other services, like Barnes & Noble's "Nook" reader and Apple's iBook reader and smaller market readers use the EPUB file format. I assume one day everyone will be standardized on the EPUB format but that hasn't happened yet. Amazon and Google have converted many classic books to digital format and there are many new books, free as well as low-cost books being developed for this format. Most traditional publishers are now publishing books both in print and in ebook formats.

Embedding

Embedding is when you take a snippet of self-contained functioning code and place it within a social media platform. For example, you can embed a widget on your website to show your recent Twitter posts. You can also embed YouTube code within your Facebook post so people can view the video on Facebook.

Engage

The act of interacting on others on social media, by posting, commenting, liking, sharing. This compares to 'lurking' which is just reading/viewing and not interacting with anyone online.

F

Facebook

A popular social networking website where users can connect with family, friends, and people of like interests, post updates on their status, or post links to interesting articles or photographs or videos. Users can also "Like" fan pages (which began for celebrities but now everyone has a fan page) as well as join groups on particular topics. Many users also participate in the many "app" games available on Facebook, including the popular Farmville.

Feed

This refers to content that is delivered in on-going intervals, in a constantly updating scrolling display. Facebook's "feed" is called a "wall." Twitter has a feed. Pinterest has a feed of visual images.

Flickr

A website where users can manage and share their photos, as well as tag and comment on photos from other users.

Follow

This is a Twitter term when users elect to "follow" other Twitter users, and then their status updates appear on your Twitter "feed" (or list of updates on your screen). You can put the users you follow into lists to make it easier to view the Twitter posts from specific groups of users. Now the term is used more broadly, in that people "follow" other people's Facebook page, their blog, their YouTube channel, etc.

FollowFriday

This is a Twitter tradition where people recommend other Twitter users to follow. These recommendations are usually posted on Fridays and you will see the tag #FollowFriday or just #FF.

Friend

In social media, 'friend' is a Facebook term of those you allow to be linked to your profile page or fan page. But it is also a more generic term for any social website of people you link to your account so that you can see their status updates, even though each site labels them slightly differently.

G

Geo-location

The term used when software on mobile devices can determine the location of the user as well as other users and businesses.

Geo-tagging

Geo-tagging is a feature on many social media websites where you can add location metadata to posts, photographs, videos, etc. Geotagging allows users to find content, businesses, services based on their proximity location.

Google Alert

This is a free service Google offers that lets you enter a keyword or phrase and every time that keyword or phrase is found on the internet, as a new addition to the Google search database, it sends you an email alert. Users use it for alerts on company names, industry terms, competitors, etc.

H

Hashtag

This is how Twitter aggregates the posts around a given topic. It is made by putting the number symbol in front of one word (even if that word is made up). So if you put in your post #MondayNightFootball, and people search on that hashtag, they will see all the posts that include that hashtag. No one can own a hashtag and people make them up. It's fun to follow trends of hashtags being used. There is even a trending list in the left column on your screen of the most popular hashtag at any given time. Hashtags are becoming so popular that I'm seeing them in Facebook posts, even though there is no hashtag feature there (but I suppose search in Facebook on a hashtag would still work in functionality). I saw one used in a magazine ad the other day. They are just the #hipthing right now.

Hyperlink

Any link on a webpage, in email, or on any social media platform that, when clicked on, redirects you to another web page on the Internet.

I

Instagram

A service now owned by Facebook that has really taken off in popularity. It allows users to take photos they've taken with their smartphone (the Instagram app currently is only available for mobile smartphones), dress it up with fun filters and effects, and then post it to any social media websites. Users can keep collections of their photos on their Instagram account, tag photos with keywords, and people can comment on them. I heard a teenager say the other day, "Oooh, I'll Instagram that." Gotta love the evolution of the English language.

J

Joomla

Joomla is a CMS (Content Management System) that allows users to build interactive websites and applications.

K

Klout

Klout is an online service that measures a person's relevance and influence on social media platforms. There is no verification of its validity but I admit to checking my Klout score every once in awhile, just to see if I'm a somebody or a nobody on their system.

L

Lifecasting

Lifecasting is when a person provides a 24x7 "feed" of their life using social media, typically making use of video feeds. Also lifecasting often includes wearing equipment, so even as they walk around, they are broadcasting their life.

Lifestreaming

This is the practice of bringing in, under one access umbrella, all the different social media activities in which a person may be participating, typically using RSS.

Like

"Like" is an action a user does on Facebook when they want to follow updates from a fan page. When a person requests to be a Friend on someone's profile page, they have to approve you before you can see their updates, but with fan pages, as soon as a user clicks the "Like" button, they'll be connected to that fan page and receive the updates on their wall of postings. Users also can not post on a fan page until they've clicked the "Like" button and link to it.

LinkedIn

A social networking site targeted specifically for working professionals, companies, and professional industry groups.

Listening

The practice of setting up searches to monitor all the social media websites for mentions of any keyword or phrases. Often used by companies to monitor what is being said about them or their products.

Live Blogging

The term used when someone is posting to their blog live from an event.

Location-Based Service

Any service on a social networking website or mobile phone application that delivers content based on the GPS (Global Positioning Service) location of the user.

Lurker

Someone who reads and watches social media content but does not actively participate.

M

Metadata

Metadata is a collection of summary information about a given media item. It typically includes things like title, description, categories, tags, but can include other items as well. YouTube uses metadata to describe videos that have been uploaded. Ebooks have metadata that describe the book's summary content.

Microblog

Any service where status update posts are limited to a small number of characters. Twitter is a microblogging website because each post on an update can only have 140 characters. Some users have made interesting use of this limitation, writing what are called Twitter Novels, posting 140 characters updates, one post at a time.

MMS

MMS stands for Multimedia Message Service. It relates to messaging on mobile smartphones. SMS are text messages sent from one mobile phone to another. MMS messages to smartphones can include images, video, and audio – not just text.

Moblog

A moblog is a blog completely updated from a mobile device.

MySpace

The social networking site that pre-dated Facebook but Facebook eventually overtook in popularity. MySpace was originally made for musicians and artists in Southern California and quickly expanded but had some missteps in the marketplace and Facebook took over as the place to be. MySpace is still active and recently ranked number 8 of all the social media websites and expected to be re-launched, completely overhauled, in the Fall of 2012.

N

Newsreader

Software that allows you to read in one location the RSS (Really Simple Syndication) input from multiple online sources. RSS is an XML-based format for sharing and distributing Web content, such as news headlines.

O

Open Source

Open Source Software (OSS) is computer software where the

source code and the right to re-work the code and build upon the code is "open" and not limited by the original developer of the software. Open source software is most commonly developed in a public collaborative fashion. The resulting product has been contributed to by many programming authors. Linux and Firefox are two examples of many example that are open-source code.

P

Permalink

This is the URL, or link, that points to a specific blog entry, particularly when it can no longer be seen on the front page and is now in the archives. It is the URL that you or others can link to in order to bring up a specific blog entry.

Phishing

"Phishing" (pronounced 'fishing') is when you get what seems to be a legit email inviting you to click a link that takes you to a website that also looks genuine. But you never arrive at the legitimate website. Instead, you end up at a URL that is slightly (or not even slightly) different from the legitimate one. The page at the bogus site looks almost identical to the legitimate one. Users not paying attention may not even notice and proceed to enter their account information and password. (see Pharming; Spy Phishing)

Pinterest

A fast-growing visual website that allows users to "pin" or bookmark photos they like on the Internet, organize them into collections, and share them with other users.

Podcast

Video or audio-based recordings that can be listened to or viewed online or downloaded to a portable media player like the iPod. Podcasts exist on a wide range of topics.

Profile

Your profile is the section of your account on any social media website where you share information about yourself. It is similar to your "About" page on a website. Your profile may include a photo of your self, a paragraph about who you are and what you like, your location, your other social media URL links, etc.

Q

QR Code

A QR (Quick Response) code is typically a black and white square box of encoded information (URLs, discount coupons, freebies, etc.) that can be read by a QR Code Scanner, mobile phones with a camera, and smartphones.

R

Re-Tweet (RT)

On Twitter, there is a choice to "re-tweet" someone's posting. By "re-tweeting," you are now sharing their post with everyone who is monitoring your wall of postings, increasing the exposure for that post. Re-tweeting is a good activity for building and enhancing relationships on Twitter.

RSS Feed

RSS stands for Really Simple Syndication. RSS allows you to subscribe to blogs, websites, social networking sites (which support RSS) and "feed" all those updates to you directly without having to go to each of those websites. You need an RSS Reader in order to read all the feeds coming in that you've subscribed to.

S

Short Code.

A short code is a number so that users have a shortcut on a mobile phone for ordering, voting on a poll, or subscribing to a service. An example might be to text the word "JOIN" to the number 999999 (but I made that up so don't actually do it).

Smart Phone

A smart phone, via its little screen, can handle more than just phone calls and text messages. It can receive video and audio and many have a function to link out to the Internet via a browser and do normal Internet activities (like check your email or post on Facebook).

SMS

SMS stands for Short Message Service. This is how one cell phone sends a text-based message to another cellphone. More popularly this is called "texting."

Social Bookmarking

Services that help you organize and categorize and share collections of different pieces of social networking information – blog posts, photos, videos, online articles, etc. One example of a social bookmarking service is del.icio.us.com.

Social Couponing

Online services that offer and deliver online coupons and vouchers to save on products and services. Two popular social couponing sites are Groupon.com and LivingSocial.com.

Sock Puppet

A sock puppet is an online identity used for purposes of deception. Previously, a sock puppet would be when one person created a false identity online in order to trash someone or a company. Now it's just used when someone creates an online personality in order to pretend to be someone other than themselves. Forums used to call them Trolls – they would create an identity and then stir up controversy just to see people get upset. Companies also create sock puppet identities in order to make it look like people love their product.

Spambot

Software that spammers use to automatically post spams to the comments area of blogs.

Spim

When a spam occurs by instant messaging like Skype or ICQ, it is known and 'spim'.

Sping

Sping is shortened term for "spam ping," and is related to blogs that use “trackbacks,” so these spam are also known as “trackback spam.” Pings go from a blog to a centralized network service (a ping server) providing notification of newly published blog posts. Spings, or ping spam, are pings that are sent from spam blogs, or are sometimes multiple pings in a short interval from a legitimate source, often tens or hundreds per minute, due to misconfigured software, or a wish to make the content coming from the source appear fresh and important.

Splog

A splog (spam blog) is a blog which the author uses to fill up with revenue-generating affiliated websites links, to increase the search engine rankings of associated sites or to simply sell links/ads. Spam blogs are usually a type of scraper site, where content is often either inauthentic text or merely stolen from other websites. These blogs usually contain a high number of links to sites associated with the creator which are often disreputable or otherwise useless websites but have lots of ads on them.

T

Tag

Tags are keywords assigned to a blog post, a social networking post, a photograph posted to a social media website, a video – so that the posts become easier to find when searched.

Tag Cloud

Tag clouds are visual representations of tag words based on

how often they have been referenced within a given article or webpage (so some words will be larger and some smaller).

Troll

A troll is a person online who goes into social media communities and intentionally posts controversial messages, just to get other people riled up, disrupt the conversation, and/or cause conflict within an online community.

Tweep

A Tweep is a person you are connected to on Twitter (from the phrase, "they are my peeps"). Not to be confused with Twirp, which is a whole different concept, and not someone you necessarily call a friend.

Tweet

This is the term assigned to a status update of 140 characters or less. It is the Twitter word for a posting.

Tweetup

This term references people who use Twitter to organize offline gatherings, whether it be planned or impromptu. Search on the hashtag #tweetup or just the phrases: tweet up, tweetup, tweet-up.

Twitter Handle

Your Twitter handle is your Twitter username. Mine is @KTMObooks.

Twitterverse

A term to describe the universe of people who use Twitter and the twitter posts that happen within that social media platform. For example, blogosphere is the universe that refers to blogs.

U

UGC

Stands for User-Generated Content. Most social media platform rely upon user-generated content.

URL

URL stands for Universal Resource Locator and represents the technical web address or link for any webpage on the Internet (example: http://www.twitter.com/KTMObooks).

URL Shortener

Twitter only allows 140 characters per post, making it challenging to post some content and then add a link. Services popped up that help people shorten their URL links. This allowed them to post the short version of the URL instead of the long version, so they fit better on Twitter. Now people use these shortened url links all over the Internet. Some examples of services that can shorten your url link for you are: bitly, goo.gl, t.co, and TinyURL.

V

Vlog

A blog that is created with video clips instead of text-based entries.

Viral

When content is shared within a single social media site or amongst various social media sites by users without any prodding or promotion, usually by "word of mouth."

W

Web 2.0

This is a phrase to refer to the second generation of the Web, which focuses more on social interaction, community, blogs, and collaboration versus the more static information/library approach of the earlier Internet, Web 1.0.

Webinar

Webinars are Internet-based lectures, workshops, seminars, or meetings which allow attendees at their computers, physically located anywhere in the world, to still be able to attend the event online.

Widget

Widgets, sometimes also called gadgets, are little sets of code that display changing information in a box which can be embedded on a website, blog or other social media page. An example of a widget is where you see sites that update the weather report on a page, or show a person's latest Twitter postings on their website.

Wi-Fi

WiFi stands for Wireless Fidelity. WiFi "hotspots" allow computers within range of the hotspot to connect to the internet. Cafes and hotels offer WiFi hotspots so customers can connect while relaxing at their establishments.

Wiki

Any website or set of pages that allows its content to be worked on collaboratively by a group. The most famous of these are Wikipedia where the public basically writes and updates the content in the online encyclopedia.

Y

Yelp

This is a website that acts as an online city guide with the strength of the site being the user reviews and recommendations.

YouTube

A very popular website where users upload and share video clips on every topic imaginable.

AUTHOR BIO

Kathleen McMahon has expertise and knowledge built upon 30 years in the hi-tech industry, including 18 years as an Internet business owner. Kathleen launched one of the first art-related websites on the Internet in 1994 and in 1995 she authored the book, "*In Search of Arts & Crafts on the Internet*". She co-founded a successful Internet advertising agency for 15 years and now provides Internet and social media consulting, speaking, and coaching services for small businesses.

Kathleen currently hosts active blogs and Facebook pages where users share their scam email experiences. When she's not writing, speaking, or consulting with her Internet clients, she can be found creating fine art, primarily California landscape paintings.

Kathleen has a growing collection of book titles, which can be found at KTMObooks.com.

If you enjoyed this book, feel free to post a review on Amazon.

Made in the USA
Monee, IL
04 November 2026

67386589R00125